MBLEx

SECRETS

Study Guide
Your Key to Exam Success

MBLEx Exam Review for the
Massage & Bodywork Licensing Examination

Dear Future Exam Success Story:

Congratulations on your purchase of our study guide. Our goal in writing our study guide was to cover the content on the test, as well as provide insight into typical test taking mistakes and how to overcome them.

Standardized tests are a key component of being successful, which only increases the importance of doing well in the high-pressure high-stakes environment of test day. How well you do on this test will have a significant impact on your future, and we have the research and practical advice to help you execute on test day.

The product you're reading now is designed to exploit weaknesses in the test itself, and help you avoid the most common errors test takers frequently make.

How to use this study guide

We don't want to waste your time. Our study guide is fast-paced and fluff-free. We suggest going through it a number of times, as repetition is an important part of learning new information and concepts.

First, read through the study guide completely to get a feel for the content and organization. Read the general success strategies first, and then proceed to the content sections. Each tip has been carefully selected for its effectiveness.

Second, read through the study guide again, and take notes in the margins and highlight those sections where you may have a particular weakness.

Finally, bring the manual with you on test day and study it before the exam begins.

Your success is our success

We would be delighted to hear about your success. Send us an email and tell us your story. Thanks for your business and we wish you continued success.

Sincerely,

Mometrix Test Preparation Team

Need more help? Check out our flashcards at: http://MometrixFlashcards.com/MBLEx

TABLE OF CONTENTS

Top 20 Test Taking Tips

1. Carefully follow all the test registration procedures
2. Know the test directions, duration, topics, question types, how many questions
3. Setup a flexible study schedule at least 3-4 weeks before test day
4. Study during the time of day you are most alert, relaxed, and stress free
5. Maximize your learning style; visual learner use visual study aids, auditory learner use auditory study aids
6. Focus on your weakest knowledge base
7. Find a study partner to review with and help clarify questions
8. Practice, practice, practice
9. Get a good night's sleep; don't try to cram the night before the test
10. Eat a well balanced meal
11. Know the exact physical location of the testing site; drive the route to the site prior to test day
12. Bring a set of ear plugs; the testing center could be noisy
13. Wear comfortable, loose fitting, layered clothing to the testing center; prepare for it to be either cold or hot during the test
14. Bring at least 2 current forms of ID to the testing center
15. Arrive to the test early; be prepared to wait and be patient
16. Eliminate the obviously wrong answer choices, then guess the first remaining choice
17. Pace yourself; don't rush, but keep working and move on if you get stuck
18. Maintain a positive attitude even if the test is going poorly
19. Keep your first answer unless you are positive it is wrong
20. Check your work, don't make a careless mistake

Anatomy and Physiology

Cell

The cell is the basic organizational unit of all living things. Each piece within a cell has a function that helps organisms grow and survive. There are many different types of cells, but cells are unique to each type of organism. The one thing that all cells have in common is a membrane, which is comparable to a semi-permeable plastic bag. The membrane is composed of phospholipids. There are also some transport holes, which are proteins that help certain molecules and ions move in and out of the cell. The cell is filled with a fluid called cytoplasm or cytosol.

Within the cell are a variety of organelles, groups of complex molecules that help a cell survive, each with its own unique membrane that has a different chemical makeup from the cell membrane. The larger the cell, the more organelles it will need to live.

Cell Structural Organization

All organisms, whether plants, animals, fungi, protists, or bacteria, exhibit structural organization on the cellular and organism level. All cells contain DNA and RNA and can synthesize proteins. Cells are the basic structural units of all organisms. All organisms have a highly organized cellular structure. Each cell consists of nucleic acids, cytoplasm, and a cell membrane. Specialized organelles such as mitochondria and chloroplasts have specific functions within the cell. In single-celled organisms, that single cell contains all of the components necessary for life. In multicellular organisms, cells can become specialized. Different types of cells can have different functions. Life begins as a single cell whether by asexual or sexual reproduction. Cells are grouped together in tissues. Tissues are grouped together in organs. Organs are grouped together in systems. An organism is a complete individual.

Nuclear Parts of a Cell

- Nucleus (pl. nuclei): This is a small structure that contains the chromosomes and regulates the DNA of a cell. The nucleus is the defining structure of eukaryotic cells, and all eukaryotic cells have a nucleus. The nucleus is responsible for the passing on of genetic traits between generations. The nucleus contains a nuclear envelope, nucleoplasm, a nucleolus, nuclear pores, chromatin, and ribosomes.
- Chromosomes: These are highly condensed, threadlike rods of DNA. Short for deoxyribonucleic acid, DNA is the genetic material that stores information about the plant or animal.
- Chromatin: This consists of the DNA and protein that make up chromosomes.
- Nucleolus: This structure contained within the nucleus consists of protein. It is small, round, does not have a membrane, is involved in protein synthesis, and synthesizes and stores RNA (ribonucleic acid).
- Nuclear envelope: This encloses the structures of the nucleus. It consists of inner and outer membranes made of lipids.
- Nuclear pores: These are involved in the exchange of material between the nucleus and the cytoplasm.
- Nucleoplasm: This is the liquid within the nucleus, and is similar to cytoplasm.

Cell Membranes

The cell membrane, also referred to as the plasma membrane, is a thin semipermeable membrane of lipids and proteins. The cell membrane isolates the cell from its external environment while still enabling the cell to communicate with that outside environment. It consists of a phospholipid bilayer, or double layer, with the hydrophilic ends of the outer layer facing the external environment, the inner layer facing the inside of the cell, and the hydrophobic ends facing each other. Cholesterol in the cell membrane adds stiffness and flexibility. Glycolipids help the cell to recognize other cells of the organisms. The proteins in the cell membrane help give the cells shape. Special proteins help the cell communicate with its external environment. Other proteins transport molecules across the cell membrane.

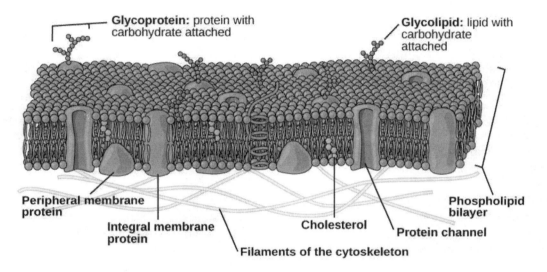

Selective Permeability

The cell membrane, or plasma membrane, has selective permeability with regard to size, charge, and solubility. With regard to molecule size, the cell membrane allows only small molecules to diffuse through it. Oxygen and water molecules are small and typically can pass through the cell membrane. The charge of the ions on the cell's surface also either attracts or repels ions. Ions with like charges are repelled, and ions with opposite charges are attracted to the cell's surface. Molecules that are soluble in phospholipids can usually pass through the cell membrane. Many molecules are not able to diffuse the cell membrane, and, if needed, those molecules must be moved through by active transport and vesicles.

Cell Structure

Ribosomes: Ribosomes are involved in synthesizing proteins from amino acids. They are numerous, making up about one-quarter of the cell. Some cells contain thousands of ribosomes. Some are mobile and some are embedded in the rough endoplasmic reticulum.

Golgi complex (Golgi apparatus): This is involved in synthesizing materials such as proteins that are transported out of the cell. It is located near the nucleus and consists of layers of membranes.

Vacuoles: These are sacs used for storage, digestion, and waste removal. There is one large vacuole in plant cells. Cells have small, sometimes numerous vacuoles.

Vesicle: This is a small organelle within a cell. It has a membrane and performs varying functions, including moving materials within a cell.

Cytoskeleton: This consists of microtubules that help shape and support the cell.

Microtubules: These are part of the cytoskeleton and help support the cell. They are made of protein.

Cytosol: This is the liquid material in the cell. It is mostly water, but also contains some floating molecules.

Cytoplasm: This is a general term that refers to cytosol and the substructures (organelles) found within the plasma membrane, but not within the nucleus.

Cell membrane (plasma membrane): This defines the cell by acting as a barrier. It helps keeps cytoplasm in and substances located outside the cell out. It also determines what is allowed to enter and exit the cell.

Endoplasmic reticulum: The two types of endoplasmic reticulum are rough (has ribosomes on the surface) and smooth (does not have ribosomes on the surface). It is a tubular network that comprises the transport system of a cell. It is fused to the nuclear membrane and extends through the cytoplasm to the cell membrane.

Mitochondrion (pl. mitochondria): These cell structures vary in terms of size and quantity. Some cells may have one mitochondrion, while others have thousands. This structure performs various functions such as generating ATP and is also involved in cell growth and death. Mitochondria contain their own DNA that is separate from that contained in the nucleus.

Mitochondria Functions
Four functions of mitochondria are: the production of cell energy, cell signaling (how communications are carried out within a cell, cellular differentiation (the process whereby a non-differentiated cell becomes transformed into a cell with a more specialized purpose), and cell cycle and growth regulation (the process whereby the cell gets ready to reproduce and reproduces). Mitochondria are numerous in eukaryotic cells. There may be hundreds or even thousands of mitochondria in a single cell. Mitochondria can be involved in many functions, their main one being supplying the cell with energy. Mitochondria consist of an inner and outer membrane. The inner membrane encloses the matrix, which contains the mitochondrial DNA (mtDNA) and ribosomes. Between the inner and outer membranes are folds (cristae). Chemical reactions occur here that release energy, control water levels in cells, and recycle and create proteins and fats. Aerobic respiration also occurs in the mitochondria.

Cell Structure
Centrosome: This is comprised of the pair of centrioles located at right angles to each other and surrounded by protein. The centrosome is involved in mitosis and the cell cycle.

Centriole: These are cylinder-shaped structures near the nucleus that are involved in cellular division. Each cylinder consists of nine groups of three microtubules. Centrioles occur in pairs.

Lysosome: This digests proteins, lipids, and carbohydrates, and also transports undigested substances to the cell membrane so they can be removed. The shape of a lysosome depends on the material being transported.

Cilia (singular: cilium): These are appendages extending from the surface of the cell, the movement of which causes the cell to move. They can also result in fluid being moved by the cell.

Flagella: These are tail-like structures on cells that use whip-like movements to help the cell move. They are similar to cilia but are usually longer and not as numerous. A cell usually only has one or a few flagella.

Cell Cycle

The term cell cycle refers to the process by which a cell reproduces, which involves cell growth, the duplication of genetic material, and cell division. Complex organisms with many cells use the cell cycle to replace cells as they lose their functionality and wear out. The entire cell cycle in animal cells can take 24 hours. The time required varies among different cell types. Human skin cells, for example, are constantly reproducing. Some other cells only divide infrequently. Once neurons are mature, they do not grow or divide. The two ways that cells can reproduce are through meiosis and mitosis. When cells replicate through mitosis, the "daughter cell" is an exact replica of the parent cell. When cells divide through meiosis, the daughter cells have different genetic coding than the parent cell. Meiosis only happens in specialized reproductive cells called gametes.

Cell Differentiation

The human body is filled with many different types of cells. The process that helps to determine the cell type of each cell is known as differentiation. Another way to say this is when a less-specialized cell becomes a more-specialized cell. This process is controlled by the genes of each cell among a group of cells known as a zygote. Following the directions of the genes, a cell builds certain proteins and other pieces that set it apart as a specific type of cell.

An example occurs with gastrulation—an early phase in the embryonic development of most animals. During gastrulation, the cells are organized into three primary germ layers: ectoderm, mesoderm, and endoderm. Then, the cells in these layers differentiate into special tissues and organs. For example, the nervous system develops from the ectoderm. The muscular system develops from the mesoderm. Much of the digestive system develops from the endoderm.

Mitosis

- The primary events that occur during mitosis are:
- Interphase: The cell prepares for division by replicating its genetic and cytoplasmic material. Interphase can be further divided into G_1, S, and G_2.
- Prophase: The chromatin thickens into chromosomes and the nuclear membrane begins to disintegrate. Pairs of centrioles move to opposite sides of the cell and spindle fibers begin to form. The mitotic spindle, formed from cytoskeleton parts, moves chromosomes around within the cell.
- Metaphase: The spindle moves to the center of the cell and chromosome pairs align along the center of the spindle structure.

- Anaphase: The pairs of chromosomes, called sisters, begin to pull apart, and may bend. When they are separated, they are called daughter chromosomes. Grooves appear in the cell membrane.
- Telophase: The spindle disintegrates, the nuclear membranes reform, and the chromosomes revert to chromatin. In animal cells, the membrane is pinched. In plant cells, a new cell wall begins to form.
- Cytokinesis: This is the physical splitting of the cell (including the cytoplasm) into two cells. Some believe this occurs following telophase. Others say it occurs from anaphase, as the cell begins to furrow, through telophase, when the cell actually splits into two.

> **Review Video: Mitosis**
> *Visit **mometrix.com/academy** and enter **Code: 849894***

Meiosis

Meiosis has the same phases as mitosis, but they happen twice. In addition, different events occur during some phases of meiosis than mitosis. The events that occur during the first phase of meiosis are interphase (I), prophase (I), metaphase (I), anaphase (I), telophase (I), and cytokinesis (I). During this first phase of meiosis, chromosomes cross over, genetic material is exchanged, and tetrads of four chromatids are formed. The nuclear membrane dissolves. Homologous pairs of chromatids are separated and travel to different poles. At this point, there has been one cell division resulting in two cells. Each cell goes through a second cell division, which consists of prophase (II), metaphase (II), anaphase (II), telophase (II), and cytokinesis (II). The result is four daughter cells with different sets of chromosomes. The daughter cells are haploid, which means they contain half the genetic material of the parent cell. The second phase of meiosis is similar to the process of mitosis. Meiosis encourages genetic diversity.

> **Review Video: Meiosis**
> *Visit **mometrix.com/academy** and enter **Code: 247334***

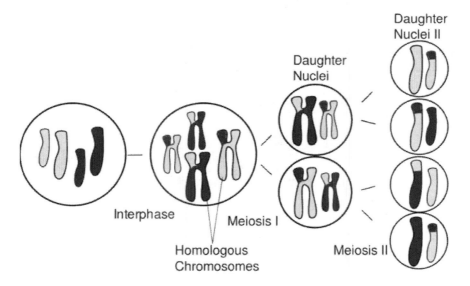

- 6 -

Tissues

Tissues are groups of cells that work together to perform a specific function. Tissues can be grouped into four broad categories: muscle tissue, nerve tissue, epithelial tissue, and connective tissue. Muscle tissue is involved in body movement. Muscle tissues can be composed of skeletal muscle cells, cardiac muscle cells, or smooth muscle cells. Skeletal muscles include the muscles commonly called biceps, triceps, hamstrings, and quadriceps. Cardiac muscle tissue is found only in the heart. Smooth muscle tissue provides tension in the blood vessels, control pupil dilation, and aid in peristalsis. Nerve tissue is located in the brain, spinal cord, and nerves. Epithelial tissue makes up the layers of the skin and various membranes. Connective tissues include bone tissue, cartilage, tendons, ligaments, fat, blood, and lymph. Tissues are grouped together as organs to form specific functions.

Categories of Tissues
Tissues may be divided into seven categories:
- Epithelial – Tissue in which cells are joined together tightly. Skin tissue is an example.
- Connective – Connective tissue may be dense, loose, or fatty. It protects and binds body parts.
- Cartilage – Cushions and provides structural support for body parts. It has a jelly-like base and is fibrous.
- Blood – Blood transports oxygen to cells and removes wastes. It also carries hormones and defends against disease.
- Bone – Bone is a hard tissue that supports and protects softer tissues and organs. Its marrow produces red blood cells.
- Muscle – Muscle tissue helps support and move the body. The three types of muscle tissue are smooth, cardiac, and skeletal.
- Nervous – Cells called neurons form a network through the body that controls responses to changes in the external and internal environment. Some send signals to muscles and glands to trigger responses.

Tissue damage, injury, or infection

The body has a number of ways to fight tissue damage, injury, and infection. The cells release proteins such as histamines and cytokines to begin the healing process. This release coincides with the constriction of blood vessels, which helps to prevent excessive bleeding. Following this, capillaries dilate to allow for the influx of white blood cells and antibodies, which fill the injured area. Platelets and fibrin aid in stopping any bleeding and in preventing any potentially harmful matter from entering the blood. They begin the clotting process, which stops the bleeding. Any pathogens are inactivated by neutrophils and macrophages. Finally, collagen enters the area to repair and mend any damaged tissues by creating scar tissue. At this point, any inflammation will have begun to subside, and this usually happens within 72 hours. Scar tissue may continue to be produced for weeks or months, depending on the severity of the injury. When there is inflammation, massage is not recommended because it impedes the healing process. After the swelling has subsided, however, massage helps to stimulate the production of scar tissue.

Tissue repair and healing
Surface tissue and skin generally require the least amount of recuperative time to heal and return to their original state. Deeper tissues, such as those within muscles, take longer to heal and require more in-depth stretching, friction, and massage techniques performed on those areas. Bones and

ligaments tend to heal slowly, while muscles and tendons heal with considerable scarring and some loss of elasticity and strength. Portions of the central nervous system that have been injured or traumatized often do not heal at all. Correct techniques for the type of injury have been shown to alleviate pain and strengthen the muscles, ligaments, and tendons, thereby decreasing the amount of scar tissue formed. The development of scar tissue is caused by connective tissue cells that have entered the area of injury and developed a fiber network. This allows regenerative tissue to bond, creating scar tissue. It is important to minimize the amount of scar tissue in any given area in order to prevent excessive buildup that can inhibit movement and range of motion.

Organs

Organs are groups of tissues that work together to perform specific functions. Complex animals have several organs that are grouped together in multiple systems. For example, the heart is specifically designed to pump blood throughout an organism's body. The heart is composed mostly of muscle tissue in the myocardium, but it also contains connective tissue in the blood and membranes, nervous tissue that controls the heart rate, and epithelial tissue in the membranes. Gills in fish and lungs in reptiles, birds, and mammals are specifically designed to exchange gasses. In birds, crops are designed to store food and gizzards are designed to grind food.

Organ systems are groups of organs that work together to perform specific functions. In mammals, there are 11 major organ systems: integumentary system, respiratory system, cardiovascular system, endocrine system, nervous system, immune system, digestive system, excretory system, muscular system, skeletal system, and reproductive system. For example, in mammals, the cardiovascular system that transports materials throughout the body consists of the heart, blood vessels, and blood. The respiratory system, which provides for the exchange of gasses, consists of the nasal passages, pharynx, larynx, trachea, bronchial tubes, lungs, alveoli, and diaphragm. The digestive system, which processes consumed food, consists of the alimentary canal and additional organs including the liver, gallbladder, and pancreas.

The Three Primary Body Planes

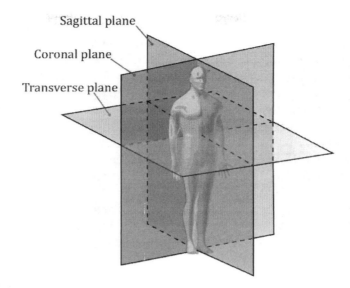

The *Transverse (or horizontal) plane* divides the patient's body into imaginary upper (superior) and lower (inferior or caudal) halves.

The *Sagittal plane* divides the body, or any body part, vertically into right and left sections. The sagittal plane runs parallel to the midline of the body.

The *Coronal (or frontal) plane* divides the body, or any body structure, vertically into front and back (anterior and posterior) sections. The coronal plane runs vertically through the body at right angles to the midline.

Terms of Direction

Medial means nearer to the midline of the body. In anatomical position, the little finger is medial to the thumb.

Lateral is the opposite of medial. It refers to structures further away from the body's midline, at the sides. In anatomical position, the thumb is lateral to the little finger.

Proximal refers to structures closer to the center of the body. The hip is proximal to the knee.

Distal refers to structures further away from the center of the body. The knee is distal to the hip.

Anterior refers to structures in front.

Posterior refers to structures behind.

Cephalad and cephalic are adverbs meaning towards the head. Cranial is the adjective, meaning of the skull.

Caudad is an adverb meaning towards the tail or posterior. Caudal is the adjective, meaning of the hindquarters.

Superior means above, or closer to the head.

Inferior means below, or closer to the feet.

Respiratory System

Structure of the Respiratory System

The respiratory system can be divided into the upper and lower respiratory system. The upper respiratory system includes the nose, nasal cavity, mouth, pharynx, and larynx. The lower respiratory system includes the trachea, lungs, and bronchial tree. Alternatively, the components of the respiratory system can be categorized as part of the airway, the lungs, or the respiratory muscles. The airway includes the nose, nasal cavity, mouth, pharynx, (throat), larynx (voice box), trachea (windpipe), bronchi, and bronchial network. The airway is lined with cilia that trap microbes and debris and sweep them back toward the mouth. The lungs are structures that house the bronchi and bronchial network, which extend into the lungs and terminate in millions of alveoli (air sacs). The walls of the alveoli are only one cell thick, allowing for the exchange of gasses with the blood capillaries that surround them. The right lung has three lobes. The left lung only has two lobes, leaving room for the heart on the left side of the body. The lungs are surrounded by a pleural membrane, which reduces friction between surfaces when breathing. The respiratory muscles include the diaphragm and the intercostal muscles. The diaphragm is a dome-shaped muscle that separates the thoracic and abdominal cavities. The intercostal muscles are located between the ribs.

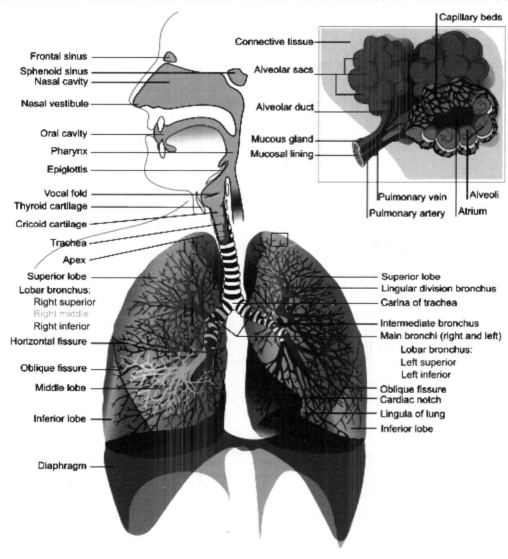

Functions of the Respiratory System

The main function of the respiratory system is to supply the body with oxygen and rid the body of carbon dioxide. This exchange of gasses occurs in millions of tiny alveoli, which are surrounded by blood capillaries. The respiratory system also filters air. Air is warmed, moistened, and filtered as it passes through the nasal passages before it reaches the lungs. The respiratory system is responsible for speech. As air passes through the throat, it moves through the larynx (voice box), which vibrates and produces sound, before it enters the trachea (windpipe). The respiratory system is vital in cough production. Foreign particles entering the nasal passages or airways are expelled from the body by the respiratory system. The respiratory system functions in the sense of smell. Chemoreceptors that are located in the nasal cavity respond to airborne chemicals. The respiratory system also helps the body maintain acid-base homeostasis. Hyperventilation can increase blood pH during acidosis (low pH). Slowing breathing during alkalosis (high pH) helps to lower blood pH.

Breathing Process

During the breathing process, the diaphragm and the intercostal muscles contract to expand the lungs. During inspiration or inhalation, the diaphragm contracts and moves down, increasing the size of the chest cavity. During expiration or exhalation, the intercostal muscles relax and the ribs contract, decreasing the size of the chest cavity. As the volume of the chest cavity increases, the pressure inside the chest cavity decreases. Because the outside air is under a greater amount of pressure than the air inside the lungs, air rushes into the lungs. When the diaphragm and intercostal muscles relax, the size of the chest cavity decreases, forcing air out of the lungs. The breathing process is controlled by the portion of the brain stem called the medulla oblongata. The medulla oblongata monitors the level of carbon dioxide in the blood and signals the breathing rate to increase when these levels are too high.

Cardiovascular System

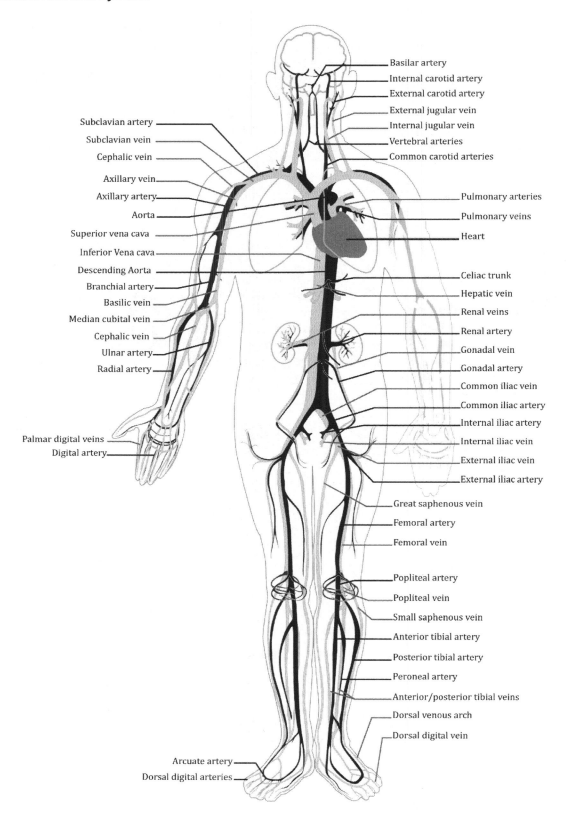

Basilar artery
Internal carotid artery
External carotid artery
External jugular vein
Internal jugular vein
Vertebral arteries
Common carotid arteries

Subclavian artery
Subclavian vein
Cephalic vein
Axillary vein
Axillary artery
Aorta
Superior vena cava
Inferior Vena cava
Descending Aorta
Branchial artery
Basilic vein
Median cubital vein
Cephalic vein
Ulnar artery
Radial artery

Pulmonary arteries
Pulmonary veins
Heart
Celiac trunk
Hepatic vein
Renal veins
Renal artery
Gonadal vein
Gonadal artery
Common iliac vein
Common iliac artery
Internal iliac artery
Internal iliac vein
External iliac vein
External iliac artery

Palmar digital veins
Digital artery

Great saphenous vein
Femoral artery
Femoral vein

Popliteal artery
Popliteal vein
Small saphenous vein
Anterior tibial artery
Posterior tibial artery
Peroneal artery
Anterior/posterior tibial veins
Dorsal venous arch
Dorsal digital vein

Arcuate artery
Dorsal digital arteries

- 12 -

The circulatory system is responsible for the internal transport of substances to and from the cells. The circulatory system usually consists of the following three parts:

- Blood – Blood is composed of water, solutes, and other elements in a fluid connective tissue.
- Blood Vessels – Tubules of different sizes that transport blood.
- Heart – The heart is a muscular pump providing the pressure necessary to keep blood flowing.

Circulatory systems can be either open or closed. Most animals have closed systems, where the heart and blood vessels are continually connected. As the blood moves through the system from larger tubules through smaller ones, the rate slows down. The flow of blood in the capillary beds, the smallest tubules, is quite slow.

A supplementary system, the lymph vascular system, cleans up excess fluids and proteins and returns them to the circulatory system.

Blood

Blood helps maintain a healthy internal environment by carrying raw materials to cells and removing waste products. It helps stabilize internal pH and hosts various kinds of infection fighters.

An adult human has about five quarts of blood. Blood is composed of red and white blood cells, platelets, and plasma. Plasma constitutes over half of the blood volume. It is mostly water and serves as a solvent. Plasma contains plasma proteins, ions, glucose, amino acids, hormones, and dissolved gasses.

Red blood cells transport oxygen to cells. Red blood cells form in the bone marrow and can live for about four months. These cells are constantly being replaced by fresh ones, keeping the total number relatively stable.

White blood cells defend the body against infection and remove various wastes. The types of white blood cells include lymphocytes, neutrophils, monocytes, eosinophils, and basophils. Platelets are fragments of stem cells and serve an important function in blood clotting.

Heart

The heart is a muscular pump made of cardiac muscle tissue. It has four chambers; each half contains both an atrium and a ventricle, and the halves are separated by a valve, known as the AV valve. It is located between the ventricle and the artery leading away from the heart. Valves keep blood moving in a single direction and prevent any backwash into the chambers.

The heart has its own circulatory system with its own coronary arteries. The heart functions by contracting and relaxing. Atrial contraction fills the ventricles and ventricular contraction empties them, forcing circulation. This sequence is called the cardiac cycle. Cardiac muscles are attached to each other and signals for contractions spread rapidly. A complex electrical system controls the heartbeat as cardiac muscle cells produce and conduct electric signals. These muscles are said to be self-exciting, needing no external stimuli.

> **Review Video: The Heart**
> Visit **mometrix.com/academy** and enter **Code: 451399**

Cardiac Cycle

The cardiac cycle consists of diastole and systole phases, which can be further divided into the first and second phases to describe the events of the right and left sides of the heart. However, these events are simultaneously occurring. During the first diastole phase, blood flows through the superior and inferior venae cavae. Because the heart is relaxed, blood flows passively from the atrium through the open atrioventricular valve (tricuspid valve) to the right ventricle. The sinoatrial (SA) node, the cardiac pacemaker located in the wall of the right atrium, generates electrical signals, which are carried by the Purkinje fibers to the rest of the atrium, stimulating it to contract and fill the right ventricle with blood. The impulse from the SA node is transmitted to the ventricle through the atrioventricular (AV) node, signaling the right ventricle to contract and initiating the first systole phase. The tricuspid valve closes, and the pulmonary semilunar valve opens. Blood is pumped out the pulmonary arteries to the lungs. Blood returning from the lungs fills the left atrium as part of the second diastole phase. The SA node triggers the mitral valve to open, and blood fills the left ventricle. During the second systole phase, the mitral valve closes and the aortic semilunar valve opens. The left ventricle contracts and blood is pumped out of the aorta to the rest of the body.

Types of Circulation

The circulatory system includes coronary circulation, pulmonary circulation, and systemic circulation. Coronary circulation is the flow of blood to the heart tissue. Blood enters the coronary arteries, which branch off the aorta, supplying major arteries, which enter the heart with oxygenated blood. The deoxygenated blood returns to the right atrium through the cardiac veins, which empty into the coronary sinus. Pulmonary circulation is the flow of blood between the heart and the lungs. Deoxygenated blood flows from the right ventricle to the lungs through pulmonary arteries. Oxygenated blood flows back to the left atrium through the pulmonary veins. Systemic circulation is the flow of blood to the entire body with the exception of coronary circulation and pulmonary circulation. Blood exits the left ventricle through the aorta, which branches into the carotid arteries, subclavian arteries, common iliac arteries, and the renal artery. Blood returns to the heart through the jugular veins, subclavian veins, common iliac veins, and renal veins, which empty into the superior and inferior venae cavae. Included in systemic circulation is portal circulation, which is the flow of blood from the digestive system to the liver and then to the heart, and renal circulation, which is the flow of blood between the heart and the kidneys.

Blood Pressure

Blood pressure is the fluid pressure generated by the cardiac cycle.

Arterial blood pressure functions by transporting oxygen-poor blood into the lungs and oxygen-rich blood to the body tissues. Arteries branch into smaller arterioles which contract and expand based on signals from the body. Arterioles are where adjustments are made in blood delivery to specific areas based on complex communication from body systems.

Capillary beds are diffusion sites for exchanges between blood and interstitial fluid. A capillary has the thinnest wall of any blood vessel, consisting of a single layer of endothelial cells.

Capillaries merge into venules which in turn merge with larger diameter tubules called veins. Veins transport blood from body tissues back to the heart. Valves inside the veins facilitate this transport. The walls of veins are thin and contain smooth muscle and also function as blood volume reserves.

Lymphatic System

The main function of the lymphatic system is to return excess tissue fluid to the bloodstream. This system consists of transport vessels and lymphoid organs. The lymph vascular system consists of lymph capillaries, lymph vessels, and lymph ducts. The major functions of the lymph vascular system are:
- The return of excess fluid to the blood.
- The return of protein from the capillaries.
- The transport of fats from the digestive tract.
- The disposal of debris and cellular waste.

Lymphoid organs include the lymph nodes, spleen, appendix, adenoids, thymus, tonsils, and small patches of tissue in the small intestine. Lymph nodes are located at intervals throughout the lymph vessel system. Each node contains lymphocytes and plasma cells. The spleen stores macrophages which help to filter red blood cells. The thymus secretes hormones and is the major site of lymphocyte production.

Spleen

The spleen is in the upper left of the abdomen. It is located behind the stomach and immediately below the diaphragm. It is about the size of a thick paperback book and weighs just over half a pound. It is made up of lymphoid tissue. The blood vessels are connected to the spleen by splenic sinuses (modified capillaries). The following peritoneal ligaments support the spleen:
The gastrolienal ligament that connects the stomach to the spleen.
The lienorenal ligament that connects the kidney to the spleen.
The middle section of the phrenicocolic ligament (connects the left colic flexure to the thoracic diaphragm).

The main functions of the spleen are to filter unwanted materials from the blood (including old red blood cells) and to help fight infections. Up to ten percent of the population has one or more accessory spleens that tend to form at the hilum of the original spleen.

Gastrointestinal System

Most digestive systems function by the following means:
- Movement – Movement mixes and passes nutrients through the system and eliminates waste.
- Secretion – Enzymes, hormones, and other substances necessary for digestion are secreted into the digestive tract.
- Digestion – Includes the chemical breakdown of nutrients into smaller units that enter the internal environment.
- Absorption – The passage of nutrients through plasma membranes into the blood or lymph and then to the body.

The human digestive system consists of the mouth, pharynx, esophagus, stomach, small and large intestine, rectum, and anus. Enzymes and other secretions are infused into the digestive system to assist the absorption and processing of nutrients. The nervous and endocrine systems control the digestive system. Smooth muscle moves the food by peristalsis, contracting and relaxing to move nutrients along.

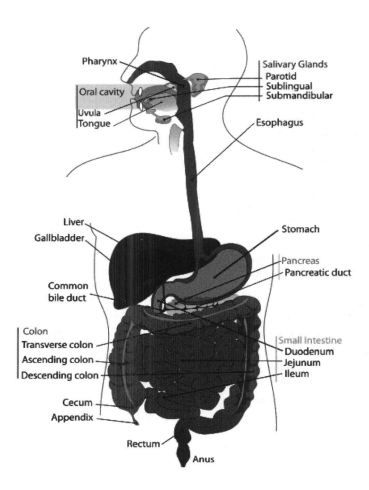

Mouth and Stomach

Digestion begins in the mouth with the chewing and mixing of nutrients with saliva. Only humans and other mammals actually chew their food. Salivary glands are stimulated and secrete saliva. Saliva contains enzymes that initiate the breakdown of starch in digestion. Once swallowed, the food moves down the pharynx into the esophagus en route to the stomach.

The stomach is a flexible, muscular sac. It has three main functions:
- Mixing and storing food
- Dissolving and degrading food via secretions
- Controlling passage of food into the small intestine

Protein digestion begins in the stomach. Stomach acidity helps break down the food and make nutrients available for absorption. Smooth muscle contractions move nutrients into the small intestine where the absorption process begins.

Liver

The liver is the largest solid organ of the body. It is also the largest gland. It weighs about three pounds and is located below the diaphragm on the right side of the chest. The liver is made up of four lobes. They are called the right, left, quadrate, and caudate lobes. The liver is secured to the diaphragm and abdominal walls by five ligaments. They are called the falciform (that forms a membrane-like barrier between the right and left lobes), coronary, right triangular, left triangular, and round ligaments. Nutrient-rich blood is supplied to the liver via the hepatic portal vein. The hepatic artery supplies oxygen-rich blood. Blood leaves the liver through the hepatic veins. The liver's functional units are called lobules (made up of layers of liver cells). Blood enters the lobules through branches of the portal vein and hepatic artery. The blood then flows through small channels called sinusoids.

The liver is responsible for performing many vital functions in the body including:
- Production of bile
- Production of certain blood plasma proteins
- Production of cholesterol (and certain proteins needed to carry fats)
- Storage of excess glucose in the form of glycogen (that can be converted back to glucose when needed)
- Regulation of amino acids.
- Processing of hemoglobin (to store iron)
- Conversion of ammonia (that is poisonous to the body) to urea (a waste product excreted in urine)
- Purification of the blood (clears out drugs and other toxins)
- Regulation of blood clotting
- Controlling infections by boosting immune factors and removing bacteria.

The liver processes all of the blood that passes through the digestive system. The nutrients (and drugs) that pass through the liver are converted into forms that are appropriate for the body to use.

Small Intestine
In the digestive process, most nutrients are absorbed in the small intestine. Enzymes from the pancreas, liver, and stomach are transported to the small intestine to aid digestion. These enzymes act on fats, carbohydrates, nucleic acids, and proteins. Bile is a secretion of the liver and is particularly useful in breaking down fats. It is stored in the gall bladder between meals.

By the time food reaches the lining of the small intestine, it has been reduced to small molecules. The lining of the small intestine is covered with villi, tiny absorptive structures that greatly increase the surface area for interaction with chime (the semi-liquid mass of partially digested food). Epithelial cells at the surface of the villi, called microvilli, further increase the ability of the small intestine to serve as the main absorption organ of the digestive tract.

Large Intestine
Also called the colon, the large intestine concentrates, mixes, and stores waste material. A little over a meter in length, the colon ascends on the right side of the abdominal cavity, cuts across transversely to the left side, then descends and attaches to the rectum, a short tube for waste disposal.

When the rectal wall is distended by waste material, the nervous system triggers an impulse in the body to expel the waste from the rectum. A muscle sphincter at the end of the anus is stimulated to facilitate the expelling of waste matter.

The speed at which waste moves through the colon is influenced by the volume of fiber and other undigested material present. Without adequate bulk in the diet, it takes longer to move waste along, sometimes with negative effects. Lack of bulk in the diet has been linked to a number of disorders.

Pancreas

The pancreas is six to ten inches long and located at the back of the abdomen behind the stomach. It is a long, tapered organ. The wider (right) side is called the head and the narrower (left) side is called the tail. The head lies near the duodenum (the first part of the small intestine) and the tail ends near the spleen. The body of the pancreas lies between the head and the tail. The pancreas is made up of exocrine and endocrine tissues. The exocrine tissue secretes digestive enzymes from a series of ducts that collectively form the main pancreatic duct (that runs the length of the pancreas). The main pancreatic duct connects to the common bile duct near the duodenum. The endocrine tissue secretes hormones (such as insulin) into the bloodstream. Blood is supplied to the pancreas from the splenic artery, gastroduodenal artery, and the superior mesenteric artery.

Digestive Role of Pancreas

The pancreas assists in the digestion of foods by secreting enzymes (to the small intestine) that help to break down many foods, especially fats and proteins. The precursors to these enzymes (called zymogens) are produced by groups of exocrine cells (called acini). They are converted, through a chemical reaction in the gut, to the active enzymes (such as pancreatic lipase and amylase) once they enter the small intestine. The pancreas also secretes large amounts of sodium bicarbonate to neutralize the stomach acid that reaches the small intestine. The exocrine functions of the pancreas are controlled by hormones released by the stomach and small intestine (duodenum) when food is present. The exocrine secretions of the pancreas flow into the main pancreatic duct (Wirsung's duct) and are delivered to the duodenum through the pancreatic duct.

Nervous System

The human nervous system senses, interprets, and issues commands as a response to conditions in the body's environment. This process is made possible by a very complex communication system organized as a grid of neurons.

Messages are sent across the plasma membrane of neurons through a process called action potential. These messages occur when a neuron is stimulated past a necessary threshold. These stimulations occur in a sequence from the stimulation point of one neuron to its contact with another neuron. At the point of contact, called a chemical synapse, a substance is released that stimulates or inhibits the action of the adjoining cell. This network fans out across the body and forms the framework for the nervous system. The direction the information flows depends on the specific organizations of nerve circuits and pathways.

Functional Types of Neurons

The three general functional types of neurons are the sensory neurons, motor neurons, and interneurons. Sensory neurons transmit signals to the central nervous system (CNS) from the sensory receptors associated with touch, pain, temperature, hearing, sight, smell, and taste. Motor neurons transmit signals from the CNS to the rest of the body such as by signaling muscles or glands to respond. Interneurons transmit signals between neurons; for example, interneurons receive transmitted signals between sensory neurons and motor neurons. In general, a neuron consists of three basic parts: the cell body, the axon, and many dendrites. The dendrites receive impulses from sensory receptors or interneurons and transmit them toward the cell body. The cell body (soma) contains the nucleus of the neuron. The axon transmits the impulses away from the cell body. The axon is insulated by oligodendrocytes and the myelin sheath with gaps known as the nodes of Ranvier. The axon terminates at the synapse.

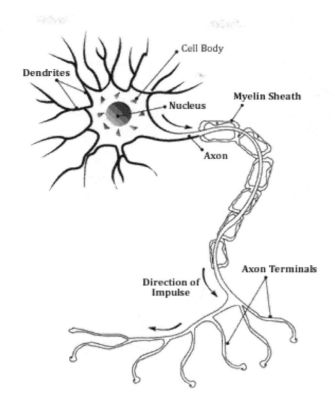

Dendrites

Cell Body

Nucleus

Myelin Sheath

Axon

Axon Terminals

Direction of Impulse

Central Nervous System

There are two primary components of the central nervous system:

Spinal Cord
The spinal cord is encased in the bony structure of the vertebrae, which protects and supports it. Its nervous tissue functions mainly with respect to limb movement and internal organ activity. Major nerve tracts ascend and descend from the spinal cord to the brain.

Brain
The brain consists of the hindbrain, which includes the medulla oblongata, cerebellum, and pons. The midbrain integrates sensory signals and orchestrates responses to these signals. The forebrain includes the cerebrum, thalamus, and hypothalamus. The cerebral cortex is a thin layer of gray matter covering the cerebrum. The brain is divided into two hemispheres, with each responsible for multiple functions.

The brain is divided into four main lobes, the frontal lobe, the parietal lobe, the occipital lobe, and the temporal lobes. The frontal lobe located in the front of the brain is responsible for a short-term and working memory and information processing as well as decision-making, planning, and judgment. The parietal lobe is located slightly toward the back of the brain and the top of the head and is responsible for sensory input as well as spatial positioning of the body. The occipital lobe is located at the back of the head just above the brain stem. This lobe is responsible for visual input, processing, and output; specifically nerves from the eyes enter directly into this lobe. Finally, the temporal lobes are located on the left and right sides of the brain. These lobes are responsible for all auditory input, processing, and output.

The cerebellum plays a role in the processing and storing of implicit memories. Specifically, for those memories developed during classical conditioning learning techniques. The role of the cerebellum was discovered by exploring the memory of individuals with damaged cerebellums. These individuals were unable to develop stimulus responses when presented via a classical conditioning technique. Researchers found that this was also the case for automatic responses. For example, when these individuals were presented with a puff or air into their eyes, they did not blink, which would have been the naturally occurring and automatic response in an individual with no brain damage.

The posterior area of the brain that is connected to the spinal cord is known as the brainstem. The midbrain, the pons, and the medulla oblongata are the three parts of the brain stem. Information from the body is sent to the brain through the brainstem, and information from the brain is sent to the body through the brainstem. The brainstem is an important part of respiratory, digestive, and circulatory functions.

The midbrain lies above the pons and the medulla oblongata. The parts of the midbrain include the tectum, the tegmentum, and the ventral tegmentum. The midbrain is an important part of vision and hearing. The pons comes between the midbrain and the medulla oblongata. Information is sent across the pons from the cerebrum to the medulla and the cerebellum. The medulla oblongata (or medulla) is beneath the midbrain and the pons. The medulla oblongata is the piece of the brain stem that connects the spinal cord to the brain. So, it has an important role in the autonomous nervous system in the circulatory and respiratory system.

In addition, the peripheral nervous system consists of the nerves and ganglia throughout the body and includes sympathetic nerves, which trigger the "fight or flight" response, and the parasympathetic nerves which control basic body function.

Autonomic Nervous System

The autonomic nervous system (ANS) maintains homeostasis within the body. In general, the ANS controls the functions of the internal organs, blood vessels, smooth muscle tissues, and glands. This is accomplished through the direction of the hypothalamus, which is located above the midbrain. The hypothalamus controls the ANS through the brain stem. With this direction from the hypothalamus, the ANS helps maintain a stable body environment (homeostasis) by regulating numerous factors including heart rate, breathing rate, body temperature, and blood pH. The ANS consists of two divisions: the sympathetic nervous system and the parasympathetic nervous system. The sympathetic nervous system controls the body's reaction to extreme, stressful, and emergency situations. For example, the sympathetic nervous system increases the heart rate, signals the adrenal glands to secrete adrenaline, triggers the dilation of the pupils, and slows digestion. The parasympathetic nervous system counteracts the effects of the sympathetic nervous system. For example, the parasympathetic nervous system decreases heart rate, signals the adrenal glands to stop secreting adrenaline, constricts the pupils, and returns the digestion process to normal.

> **Review Video: Nervous System**
*Visit **mometrix.com/academy** and enter **Code: 708428***

The Somatic Nervous system and the Reflex Arc

The somatic nervous system (SNS) controls the five senses and the voluntary movement of skeletal muscle. So, this system has all of the neurons that are connected to sense organs. Efferent (motor) and afferent (sensory) nerves help the somatic nervous system operate the senses and the movement of skeletal muscle. Efferent muscles bring signals from the central nervous system to the sensory organs and the muscles. Afferent muscles bring signals from the sensory organs and the muscles to the central nervous system. The somatic nervous system also performs involuntary movements which are known as reflex arcs.

A reflex, the simplest act of the nervous system, is an automatic response without any conscious thought to a stimulus via the reflex arc. The reflex arc is the simplest nerve pathway, which bypasses the brain and is controlled by the spinal cord. For example, in the classic knee-jerk response (patellar tendon reflex), the stimulus is the reflex hammer hitting the tendon, and the response is the muscle contracting, which jerks the foot upward. The stimulus is detected by sensory receptors, and a message is sent along a sensory (afferent) neuron to one or more interneurons in the spinal cord. The interneuron(s) transmit this message to a motor (efferent) neuron, which carries the message to the correct effector (muscle).

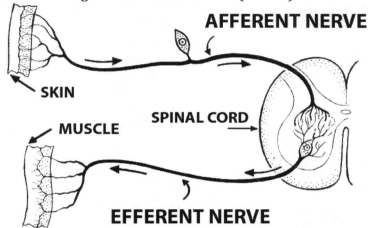

Muscular System

There are three types of muscle tissue: skeletal, cardiac, and smooth. There are over 600 muscles in the human body. All muscles have these three properties in common:
- Excitability – All muscle tissues have an electric gradient which can reverse when stimulated.
- Contraction – All muscle tissues have the ability to contract, or shorten.
- Elongate – All muscle tissues share the capacity to elongate, or relax.

Types of Muscular Tissue
The three types of muscular tissue are skeletal muscle, smooth muscle, and cardiac muscle. Skeletal muscles are voluntary muscles that work in pairs to move various parts of the skeleton. Skeletal muscles are composed of muscle fibers (cells) that are bound together in parallel bundles. Skeletal muscles are also known as striated muscle due to their striped appearance under a microscope. Smooth muscle tissues are involuntary muscles that are found in the walls of internal organs such as the stomach, intestines, and blood vessels. Smooth muscle tissues or visceral tissue is nonstriated. Smooth muscle cells are shorter and wider than skeletal muscle fibers. Smooth muscle tissue is also found in sphincters or valves that control various openings throughout the body. Cardiac muscle tissue is involuntary muscle that is found only in the heart. Like skeletal muscle cells, cardiac muscle cells are also striated.

Only skeletal muscle interacts with the skeleton to move the body. When they contract, the muscles transmit force to the attached bones. Working together, the muscles and bones act as a system of levers which move around the joints. A small contraction of a muscle can produce a large movement. A limb can be extended and rotated around a joint due to the way the muscles are arranged.

Skeletal Muscle Contraction
Skeletal muscles consist of numerous muscle fibers. Each muscle fiber contains a bundle of myofibrils, which are composed of multiple repeating contractile units called sarcomeres. Myofibrils contain two protein microfilaments: a thick filament and a thin filament. The thick filament is composed of the protein myosin. The thin filament is composed of the protein actin. The dark bands (striations) in skeletal muscles are formed when thick and thin filaments overlap. Light bands occur where the thin filament is overlapped. Skeletal muscle attraction occurs when the thin filaments slide over the thick filaments shortening the sarcomere. When an action potential (electrical signal) reaches a muscle fiber, calcium ions are released. According to the sliding filament model of muscle contraction, these calcium ions bind to the myosin and actin, which assists in the binding of the myosin heads of the thick filaments to the actin molecules of the thin filaments. Adenosine triphosphate released from glucose provides the energy necessary for the contraction.

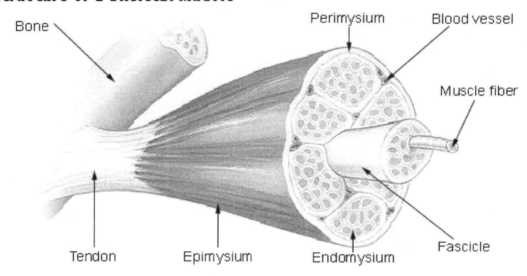

Structure of a Skeletal Muscle

Bone, Perimysium, Blood vessel, Muscle fiber, Tendon, Epimysium, Endomysium, Fascicle

Reproductive System

Male Reproductive System
The functions of the male reproductive system are to produce, maintain, and transfer sperm and semen into the female reproductive tract and to produce and secrete male hormones. The external structure includes the penis, scrotum, and testes. The penis, which contains the urethra, can fill with blood and become erect, enabling the deposition of semen and sperm into the female reproductive tract during sexual intercourse. The scrotum is a sack of skin and smooth muscle that houses the testes and keeps the testes at the proper temperature for spermatogenesis. The testes, or testicles, are the male gonads, which produce sperm and testosterone. The internal structure includes the epididymis, vas deferens, ejaculatory ducts, urethra, seminal vesicles, prostate gland, and bulbourethral glands. The epididymis stores the sperm as it matures. Mature sperm moves from the epididymis through the vas deferens to the ejaculatory duct. The seminal vesicles secrete alkaline fluids with proteins and mucus into the ejaculatory duct, also. The prostate gland secretes a milky

white fluid with proteins and enzymes as part of the semen. The bulbourethral, or Cowper's, glands secrete a fluid into the urethra to neutralize the acidity in the urethra. Additionally, the hormones associated with the male reproductive system include follicle-stimulating hormone, which stimulates spermatogenesis; luteinizing hormone, which stimulates testosterone production; and testosterone, which is responsible for the male sex characteristics.

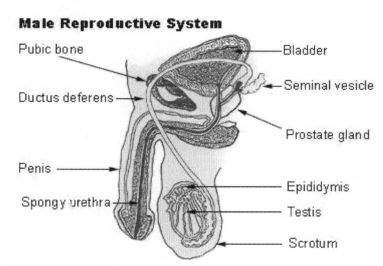

Male Reproductive System

Female Reproductive System

The functions of the female reproductive system are to produce ova (oocytes, or egg cells), transfer the ova to the fallopian tubes for fertilization, receive the sperm from the male, and to provide a protective, nourishing environment for the developing embryo. The external portion of the female reproductive system includes the labia majora, labia minora, Bartholin's glands and clitoris. The labia majora and the labia minora enclose and protect the vagina. The Bartholin's glands secrete a lubricating fluid. The clitoris contains erectile tissue and nerve endings for sensual pleasure. The internal portion of the female reproductive system includes the ovaries, fallopian tubes, uterus, and vagina. The ovaries, which are the female gonads, produce the ova and secrete estrogen and progesterone. The fallopian tubes carry the mature egg toward the uterus. Fertilization typically occurs in the fallopian tubes. If fertilized, the egg travels to the uterus, where it implants in the uterine wall. The uterus protects and nourishes the developing embryo until birth. The vagina is a muscular tube that extends from the cervix of the uterus to the outside of the body. The vagina receives the semen and sperm during sexual intercourse and provides a birth canal when needed.

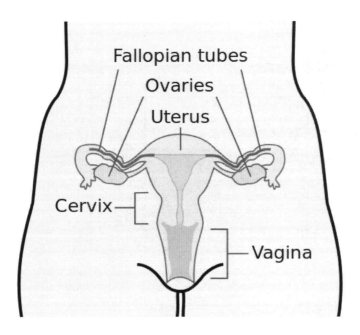

Integumentary System

The integumentary system, which consists of the skin including the sebaceous glands sweat glands, hair, and nails, serves a variety of functions associated with protection, secretion, and communication. In the functions associated with protection, the integumentary system protects the body from pathogens including bacteria, viruses, and various chemicals from entering the body. In the functions associated with secretion, sebaceous glands secrete sebum (oil) that waterproofs the skin, and sweat glands are associated with the body's homeostatic relationship of thermoregulation. Sweat glands also serve as excretory organs and help rid the body of metabolic wastes. In the functions associated with communication, sensory receptors distributed throughout the skin send information to the brain regarding pain, touch, pressure, and temperature. In addition to protection, secretion, and communication, the skin manufactures vitamin D and can absorb certain chemicals such as specific medications.

<u>Layers of the Skin</u>
The layers of the skin from the surface of the skin inward are the epidermis and dermis. The subcutaneous layer lying below the dermis is also part of the integumentary system. The epidermis is the most superficial layer of the skin. The epidermis, which consists entirely of epithelial cells, does not contain any blood vessels. The deepest portion of the epidermis is the stratum basale, which is a single layer of cells that continually undergo division. As more and more cells are produced, older cells are pushed toward the surface. Most epidermal cells are keratinized. Keratin is a waxy protein that helps to waterproof the skin. As the cells die, they are sloughed off. The dermis lies directly beneath the epidermis. The dermis consists mostly of connective tissue. The dermis contains blood vessels, sensory receptors, hair follicles, sebaceous glands, and sweat glands. The dermis also contains elastin and collagen fibers. The subcutaneous layer or hypodermis is actually not a layer of the skin. The subcutaneous layer consists of connective tissue, which binds the skin to the underlying muscles. Fat deposits in the subcutaneous layer help to cushion and insulate the body.

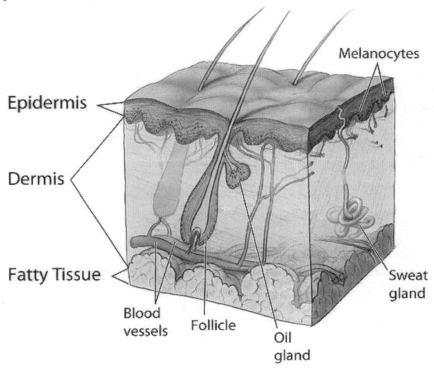

<u>Skin's Involvement in Temperature Homeostasis</u>
The skin is involved in temperature homeostasis or thermoregulation through the activation of the sweat glands. By thermoregulation, the body maintains a stable body temperature as one component of a stable internal environment. The temperature of the body is controlled by a negative feedback system consisting of a receptor, control center, and effector. The receptors are sensory cells located in the dermis of the skin. The control center is the hypothalamus, which is located in the brain. The effectors include the sweat glands, blood vessels, and muscles (shivering). The evaporation of sweat from the surface of the skin cools the body to maintain its tolerance range. Vasodilation of the blood vessels near the surface of the skin also releases heat into the environment to lower body temperature. Shivering is associated with the muscular system.

Sebaceous Glands vs. Sweat Glands

Sebaceous glands and sweat glands are exocrine glands found in the skin. Exocrine glands secrete substances into ducts. In this case, the secretions are through the ducts to the surface of the skin. Sebaceous glands are holocrine glands, which secrete sebum. Sebum is an oily mixture of lipids and proteins. Sebaceous glands are connected to hair follicles and secrete sebum through the hair pore. Sebum inhibits water loss from the skin and protects against bacterial and fungal infections. Sweat glands are either eccrine glands or apocrine glands. Eccrine glands are not connected to hair follicles. They are activated by elevated body temperature. Eccrine glands are located throughout the body and can be found on the forehead, neck, and back. Eccrine glands secrete a salty solution of electrolytes and water containing sodium chloride, potassium, bicarbonate, glucose, and antimicrobial peptides.

Eccrine glands are activated as part of the body's thermoregulation. Apocrine glands secrete an oily solution containing fatty acids, triglycerides, and proteins. Apocrine glands are located in the armpits, groin, palms, and soles of the feet. Apocrine glands secrete this oily sweat when a person experiences stress or anxiety. Bacteria feed on apocrine sweat and expel aromatic fatty acids, producing body odor.

Endocrine System

The endocrine system is responsible for secreting the hormones and other molecules that help regulate the entire body in both the short and the long term. There is a close working relationship between the endocrine system and the nervous system. The hypothalamus and the pituitary gland coordinate to serve as a neuroendocrine control center.

Hormone secretion is triggered by a variety of signals, including hormonal signs, chemical reactions, and environmental cues. Only cells with particular receptors can benefit from hormonal influence. This is the "key in the lock" model for hormonal action. Steroid hormones trigger gene activation and protein synthesis in some target cells. Protein hormones change the activity of existing enzymes in target cells. Hormones such as insulin work quickly when the body signals an urgent need. Slower acting hormones afford longer, gradual, and sometimes permanent changes in the body.

The eight major endocrine glands and their functions are:
- Adrenal cortex – Monitors blood sugar level; helps in lipid and protein metabolism.
- Adrenal medulla – Controls cardiac function; raises blood sugar and controls the size of blood vessels.
- Thyroid gland – Helps regulate metabolism and functions in growth and development.
- Parathyroid – Regulates calcium levels in the blood.
- Pancreas islets – Raises and lowers blood sugar; active in carbohydrate metabolism.
- Thymus gland – Plays a role in immune responses.
- Pineal gland – Has an influence on daily biorhythms and sexual activity.
- Pituitary gland – Plays an important role in growth and development.

Endocrine glands are intimately involved in a myriad of reactions, functions, and secretions that are crucial to the well-being of the body.

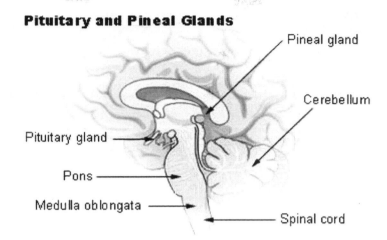

Pituitary and Pineal Glands

Endocrine Functions of the Pancreas
Located amongst the groupings of exocrine cells (acini) are groups of endocrine cells (called islets of Langerhans). The islets of Langerhans are primarily made up of insulin-producing beta cells (fifty to eighty percent of the total) and glucagon-releasing alpha cells. The major hormones produced by the pancreas are insulin and glucagon. The body uses insulin to control carbohydrate metabolism by lowering the amount of sugar (glucose) in the blood. Insulin also affects fat metabolism and can change the liver's ability to release stored fat. The body also uses glucagon to control carbohydrate metabolism. Glucagon has the opposite effect of insulin in that the body uses it to increase blood sugar (glucose) levels. The levels of insulin and glucagon are balanced to maintain the optimum level of blood sugar (glucose) throughout the day.

Thyroid and Parathyroid Glands
The thyroid and parathyroid glands are located in the neck just below the larynx. The parathyroid glands are four small glands that are embedded on the posterior side of the thyroid gland. The basic function of the thyroid gland is to regulate metabolism. The thyroid gland secretes the hormones thyroxine, triiodothyronine, and calcitonin. Thyroxine and triiodothyronine increase metabolism and calcitonin decreases blood calcium by storing calcium in bone tissue. The hypothalamus directs the pituitary gland to secrete thyroid-stimulating hormone (TSH), which stimulates the thyroid gland to release these hormones as needed via a negative-feedback mechanism. The parathyroid glands secrete parathyroid hormone, which can increase blood calcium by moving calcium from the bone to the blood.

Renal/Urinary System

The renal/urinary system is capable of eliminating excess substances while preserving the substances needed by the body to function. The urinary system consists of the kidneys, urinary ducts, and bladder. The mammalian kidney is a bean-shaped organ attached to the body near the peritoneum. The kidney helps to eliminate water and waste from the body. Within the kidney, there are various tubes and capillaries. Substances exit the bloodstream if they are not needed, and those that are needed are reabsorbed. The unnecessary substances are filtered out into the tubules that form urine. From theses tubes, urine flows into the bladder and then out of the body through the urethra.

Components of the Urinary System

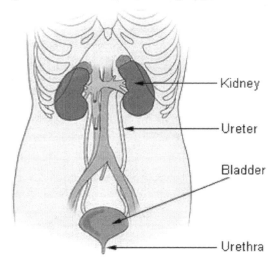

Kidney

Ureter

Bladder

Urethra

Kidneys
The kidneys are bean-shaped structures that are located at the back of the abdominal cavity just under the diaphragm. Each kidney consists of three layers: the renal cortex (outer layer), renal medulla (inner layer), and renal pelvis (innermost portion). The renal cortex is composed of approximately one million nephrons, which are the tiny, individual filters of the kidneys. Each nephron contains a cluster of capillaries called a glomerulus surrounded by the cup-shaped Bowman's capsule, which leads to a tubule. The kidneys receive blood from the renal arteries, which branch off the aorta.

In general, the kidneys filter the blood, reabsorb needed materials, and secrete wastes and excess water in the urine. More specifically, blood flows from the renal arteries into arterioles into the glomerulus, where it is filtered. The glomerular filtrate enters the proximal convoluted tubule where water, glucose, ions, and other organic molecules are resorbed back into the bloodstream. Additional substances such as urea and drugs are removed from the blood in the distal convoluted tubule. Also, the pH of the blood can be adjusted in the distal convoluted tubule by the secretion of hydrogen ions. Finally, the unabsorbed materials flow out from the collecting tubules located in the renal medulla to the renal pelvis as urine. Urine is drained from the kidneys through the ureters to the urinary bladder, where it is stored until expulsion from the body through the urethra.

Immune System

The immune system protects the body against invading pathogens including bacteria, viruses, fungi, and protists. The immune system includes the lymphatic system (lymph, lymph capillaries, lymph vessel, and lymph nodes) as well as the red bone marrow and numerous leukocytes, or white blood cells. Tissue fluid enters the lymph capillaries, which combine to form lymph vessels. Skeletal muscle contractions move the lymph one way through the lymphatic system to lymphatic ducts, which dump back into the venous blood supply into the lymph nodes, which are situated along the lymph vessels, and filter the lymph of pathogens and other matter. The lymph nodes are concentrated in the neck, armpits, and groin areas. Outside the lymphatic vessel system lies the lymphatic tissue including the tonsils, adenoids, thymus, spleen, and Peyer's patches. The tonsils, located in the pharynx, protect against pathogens entering the body through the mouth and throat. The thymus serves as a maturation chamber for the immature T cells that are formed in the bone marrow. The spleen cleans the blood of dead cells and pathogens. Peyer's patches, which are located in the small intestine, protect the digestive system from pathogens.

The body's general immune defenses include:
- Skin – An intact epidermis and dermis form a formidable barrier against bacteria.
- Ciliated Mucous Membranes – Cilia sweep pathogens out of the respiratory tract.
- Glandular Secretions – Secretions from exocrine glands destroy bacteria.
- Gastric Secretions – Gastric acid destroys pathogens.
- Normal Bacterial Populations – Compete with pathogens in the gut and vagina.

In addition, phagocytes and inflammation responses mobilize white blood cells and chemical reactions to stop infection. These responses include localized redness, tissue repair, and fluid-seeping healing agents. Additionally, plasma proteins act as the complement system to repel bacteria and pathogens.

Three types of white blood cells form the foundation of the body's immune system. They are:
- Macrophages – Phagocytes that alert T cells to the presence of foreign substances.
- T Lymphocytes – These directly attack cells infected by viruses and bacteria.
- B Lymphocytes – These cells target specific bacteria for destruction.

Memory cells, suppressor T cells, and helper T cells also contribute to the body's defense. Immune responses can be antibody mediated when the response is to an antigen, or cell-mediated when the response is to already infected cells. These responses are controlled and measured counter-attacks that recede when the foreign agents are destroyed. If an invader returns after it has attacked the body, it is immediately recognized and a secondary immune response occurs. This secondary response is rapid and powerful, much more so than the original response. These memory lymphocytes circulate throughout the body for years, alert to a possible new attack.

Types of Leukocytes
Leukocytes, or white blood cells, are produced in the red bone marrow. Leukocytes can be classified as monocytes (macrophages and dendritic cells), granulocytes (neutrophils, basophils, and eosinophils), T lymphocytes, B lymphocytes, or natural killer cells. Macrophages found traveling in the lymph or fixed in lymphatic tissue are the largest, long-living phagocytes that engulf and destroy pathogens. Dendritic cells present antigens (foreign particles) to T cells. Neutrophils are short-living phagocytes that respond quickly to invaders. Basophils alert the body of invasion. Eosinophils are large, long-living phagocytes that defend against multicellular invaders. T lymphocytes or T cells include helper T cells, killer T cells, suppressor T cells, and memory T cells. Helper T cells help the body fight infections by producing antibodies and other chemicals. Killer T cells destroy cells that are infected with a virus or pathogen and tumor cells. Suppressor T cells stop or "suppress" the other T cells when the battle is over. Memory T cells remain in the blood on alert in case the invader attacks again. B lymphocytes, or B cells, produce antibodies.

Antigen and Typical Immune Response
Antigens are substances that stimulate the immune system. Antigens are typically proteins on the surfaces of bacteria, viruses, and fungi. Substances such as drugs, toxins, and foreign particles can

also be antigens. The human body recognizes the antigens of its own cells, but it will attack cells or substances with unfamiliar antigens. Specific antibodies are produced for each antigen that enters the body. In a typical immune response, when a pathogen or foreign substance enters the body, it is engulfed by a macrophage, which presents fragments of the antigen on its surface. A helper T cell joins the macrophage, and the killer (cytotoxic) T cells and B cells are activated. Killer T-cells search out and destroy cells presenting the same antigens. B cells differentiate into plasma cells and memory cells. Plasma cells produce antibodies specific to that pathogen or foreign substance. Antibodies bind to antigens on the surface of pathogens and mark them for destruction by other phagocytes. Memory cells remain in the bloodstream to protect against future infections from the same pathogen.

Active and Passive Immunity
At birth, an innate immune system protects an individual from pathogens. When an individual encounters infection or has an immunization, the individual develops an adaptive immunity that reacts to pathogens. So, this adaptive immunity is acquired. Active and passive immunities can be acquired naturally or artificially.

A naturally acquired active immunity is natural because the individual is exposed and builds immunity to a pathogen without an immunization. An artificially acquired active immunity is artificial because the individual is exposed and builds immunity to a pathogen by a vaccine.

A naturally acquired passive immunity is natural because it happens during pregnancy as antibodies move from the mother's bloodstream to the bloodstream of the fetus. The antibodies can also be transferred from a mother's breast milk. During infancy, these antibodies provide temporary protection until childhood. An artificially acquired passive immunity is an immunization that is given in recent outbreaks or emergency situations. This immunization provides quick and short-lived protection to disease by the use of antibodies that can come from another person or animal.

Skeletal System

The skeletal structure in humans contains both bones and cartilage. Over 200 bones in the human body can be divided into two parts:
- Axial skeleton – Includes the skull, sternum, ribs, and vertebral column (the spine).
- Appendicular skeleton – Includes the bones of the arms, feet, hands, legs, hips, and shoulders.

Adult Human Skeleton

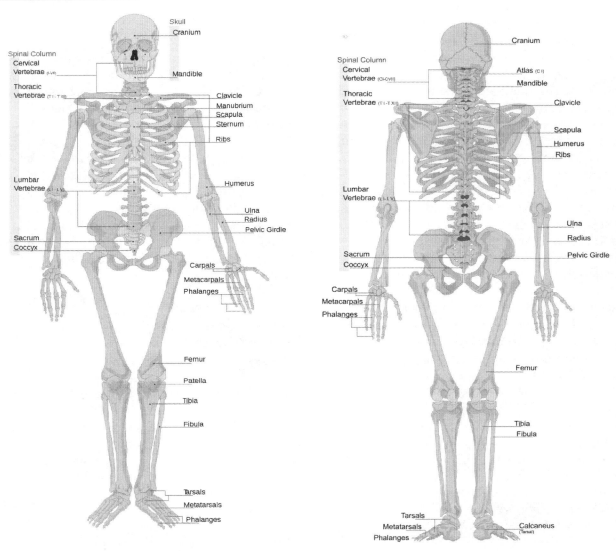

Axial Skeleton and the Appendicular Skeleton

The human skeletal system, which consists of 206 bones along with numerous tendons, ligaments, and cartilage, is divided into the axial skeleton and the appendicular skeleton. The axial skeleton consists of 80 bones and includes the vertebral column, rib cage, sternum, skull, and hyoid bone. The vertebral column consists of 33 vertebrae classified as cervical vertebrae, thoracic vertebrae, lumbar vertebrae, and sacral vertebrae. The rib cage includes 12 paired ribs, 10 pairs of true ribs and 2 pairs of floating ribs, and the sternum, which consists of the manubrium, corpus sterni, and xiphoid process. The skull includes the cranium and facial bones. The ossicles are bones in the middle ear. The hyoid bone provides an attachment point for the tongue muscles. The axial skeleton protects vital organs including the brain, heart, and lungs. The appendicular skeleton consists of 126 bones including the pectoral girdle, pelvic girdle, and appendages. The pectoral girdle consists of the scapulae (shoulders) and clavicles (collarbones). The pelvic girdle consists of two pelvic (hip) bones, which attach to the sacrum. The upper appendages (arms) include the humerus, radius, ulna, carpals, metacarpals, and phalanges. The lower appendages (legs) include the femur, patella, fibula, tibia, tarsals, metatarsals, and phalanges.

Functions of the Skeletal System
The skeletal system serves many functions including providing structural support, providing movement, providing protection, producing blood cells, and storing substances such as fat and minerals. The skeletal system provides the body with structure and support for the muscles and organs. The axial skeleton transfers the weight from the upper body to the lower appendages. The skeletal system provides movement with joints and the muscular system. Bones provide attachment points for muscles. Joints including hinge joints, ball-and-socket joints, pivot joints, ellipsoid joints, gliding joints, and saddle joints. Each muscle is attached to two bones: the origin and the insertion. The origin remains immobile, and the insertion is the bone that moves as the muscle contracts and relaxes. The skeletal system serves to protect the body. The cranium protects the brain. The vertebrae protect the spinal cord. The rib cage protects the heart and lungs. The pelvis protects the reproductive organs. The red marrow manufactures red and white blood cells. All bone marrow is red at birth, but adults have approximately one-half red bone marrow and one-half yellow bone marrow. Yellow bone marrow stores fat. Also, the skeletal system provides a reservoir to store the minerals calcium and phosphorus.

The skeletal system has an important role in the following body functions:
- Movement – The action of skeletal muscles on bones moves the body.
- Mineral Storage – Bones serve as storage facilities for essential mineral ions.
- Support – Bones act as a framework and support system for the organs.
- Protection – Bones surround and protect key organs in the body.
- Blood Cell Formation – Red blood cells are produced in the marrow of certain bones.

Bones are classified as long, short, flat, or irregular. They are a connective tissue with a base of pulp containing collagen and living cells. Red marrow, an important site of red blood cell production, fills the spongy tissue of many bones. Bone tissue is constantly regenerating itself as the mineral composition changes. This allows for special needs during growth periods and maintains calcium levels for the body. Bone regeneration can deteriorate in old age, particularly among women, leading to osteoporosis.

The flexible and curved backbone is supported by muscles and ligaments. Intervertebral discs are stacked one above another and provide cushioning for the backbone. Trauma or shock may cause these discs to herniate and cause pain. The sensitive spinal cord is enclosed in a cavity which is well protected by the bones of the vertebrae.

Joints are areas of contact adjacent to bones. Synovial joints are the most common and are freely movable. These may be found at the shoulders and knees. Cartilaginous joints fill the spaces between some bones and restrict movement. Examples of cartilaginous joints are those between vertebrae. Fibrous joints have fibrous tissue connecting bones and no cavity is present.

Compact and Spongy Bone

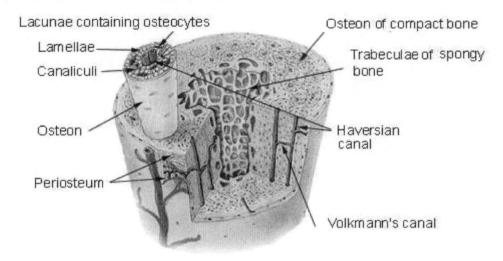

Compact Bone & Spongy (Cancellous) Bone

Lacunae containing osteocytes
Lamellae
Canaliculi
Osteon
Periosteum
Osteon of compact bone
Trabeculae of spongy bone
Haversian canal
Volkmann's canal

Two types of connective bone tissue include compact bone and spongy bone. Compact, or cortical, bone, which consists of tightly packed cells, is strong, dense, and rigid. Running vertically throughout compact bone are the Haversian canals, which are surrounded by concentric circles of bone tissue called lamellae. The spaces between the lamellae are called the lacunae. These lamellae and canals along with their associated arteries, veins, lymph vessels, and nerve endings are referred to collectively as the Haversian system. The Haversian system provides a reservoir for calcium and phosphorus for the blood. Also, bones have a thin outside layer of compact bone, which gives them their characteristic smooth, white appearance. Spongy, or cancellous, bone consists of trabeculae, which are a network of girders with open spaces filled with red bone marrow. Compared to compact bone, spongy bone is lightweight and porous, which helps reduce the bone's overall weight. The red marrow manufactures red and white blood cells. In long bones, the diaphysis consists of compact bone surrounding the marrow cavity and spongy bone containing red marrow in the epiphyses. Bones have varying amounts of compact bone and spongy bone depending on their classification.

Special senses

The special senses are vision, hearing, smell, and taste (touch is described as a somatic sense). The visual system consists of the eyes and a series of nerves connecting the eyes to the brain. The external surface of the eye is composed of the lens, which is surrounded by the iris and covered by the cornea. The hearing system consists of the ear and the central auditory system. The system of smell, commonly known as the olfactory sense, is composed of various olfactory receptors in the nose, which transmit information about odors to the brain. The primary structure of the taste system is the tongue, which contains sensory receptors for the following kinds of tastes: sour, sweet, salty, savory, and bitter.

The senses are used to acquire information about the internal and external world of the person. The sense of sight is probably the most important of the special senses for human beings. It functions by allowing light to pass through the lens and hit the retina, after which the image is transmitted along the optic nerve to the brain. The sense of hearing basically functions as follows: sound waves are received through the ear. They vibrate the eardrum and then pass through a series of tubes, from which information is then transmitted to the brain through various auditory nerves. The system of taste depends on chemical reactions between receptors in the mouth and other materials, such as food and drink.

Kinesiology

Muscle tissue

The purpose of muscle tissue is to contract the fibers that compose the muscles, which allows the body to move. The first type of muscle tissue is skeletal muscle. Tendons attach these muscles to the bones. Movement of these muscles is controlled through conscious effort. Impulses are sent from the brain and travel through the nerves to the muscle. Because of the manner in which impulses are transmitted, these skeletal muscles are referred to as voluntary muscles. The cells of these muscles are long and resemble threads. They contain dark and light markings known as striations. These types of muscles are known as striated muscles. The second type of muscle tissue is smooth muscle. Generally, this type is non-striated and cannot be controlled or made to contract through voluntary means. Food is transported through the digestive tract with the aid of smooth muscles. The third type of muscle tissue is cardiac muscle tissue, which is found only in the heart. It functions involuntarily and helps to pump blood throughout the body via the arteries and veins through cardiac contractions.

<u>Composition of skeletal muscle tissue</u>
Skeletal muscle tissue is composed of fibrous tissue arranged in bundles called fascicles. These fascicles are made up of muscle fibers connected to one another through connective tissue. An extensive supply of blood and lymph vessels, capillaries, and nerve fibers are contained within skeletal muscle tissue. The muscle receives its supply of oxygen through the blood vessels. There are two types of skeletal muscle fibers: type I and type II. Type I muscle fibers are characterized by a large number of reddish fibers, which provide excellent endurance for the muscle through oxidative metabolism. Type II fibers are white in color, and are more suitable for shorter bursts of energy or when speed is required. They rely on anaerobic metabolism for energy and tire more easily. The composition of an individual's skeletal muscle tissue is determined by genetics and by the type of exercise they do on a regular basis.

<u>Structure of muscle tissue</u>
Muscle tissue is made up of bundles of fibers that are held in position and separated by various partitions. These partitions range from large (deep fascia, epimysium) to small (perimysium, endomysium), and often extend beyond the entire length of the muscle and form tendon, which is connected to another bone. Each muscle cell is extremely long and has a large number of nuclei. Every muscle cell contains a number of smaller units called sarcomeres; these contain thick filaments of the protein myosin and thin filaments of the protein actin. Muscle tissue contracts when a nerve stimulates the muscle and the thin filaments compress within the sarcomere, causing a general muscle contraction.

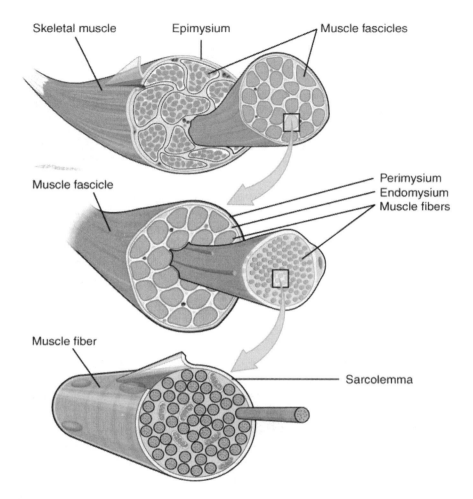

Skeletal muscle — Epimysium — Muscle fascicles

Muscle fascicle — Perimysium, Endomysium, Muscle fibers

Muscle fiber — Sarcolemma

Muscle shapes

The muscles of the human body can be numerous shapes, depending on their function. In the trapezius, for instance, the muscle fibers are arranged in a broad, flat pattern, and attach at a large number of points along the scapula. The bicep, on the other hand, is a long, narrow muscle. The muscles of the deep back are very short and appear as knotty bundles along the spinal column. Longer muscles are generally capable of producing highly visible external movements and are used to transport heavy objects, for example. Small, deep muscles are usually responsible for precise, balancing adjustments. Muscles that only cross over one joint are called monoarticular, while those that extend across and move more than one joint are called polyarticular.

Isometric and isotonic contractions

When reviewing the ways that muscles contract and expand, it is important to note the differences between the two types of muscle contractions. An isometric contraction occurs when the muscle is contracting, but no increase in the length of the muscle is observed. The muscle being isolated is tensed, but the corresponding body part does not move. An isotonic contraction occurs when the muscle contracts and the distance from one end of the muscle to the other changes. The majority of the body's voluntary movements are considered isotonic. Isometric contractions are responsible for keeping the body in an upright position. An isometric contraction occurs when a person pushes extremely hard against a heavy object but is not able to move it. The tension felt within the body is considered an isometric contraction. When a person is engaged in regular physical exercise, such as running, the muscle contractions that occur are isotonic.

Muscle attachments

In most cases, a muscle is attached to two different bones. When the body moves, the origin bone will be fixed in some way, while the other bone (known as the insertion bone) moves because of a muscle contraction. Occasionally, health professionals will refer to the origin bone as the proximal bone. Although the only voluntary motion a muscle is capable of is contraction, muscles are generally elastic in nature, meaning that muscles stretched beyond their normal length will usually return to their original size. This is part of the reason why the body has a general tendency to retain a particular shape. Muscles can be attached to bones by tendons or muscle fibers.

Functions of muscles

Muscles are able to perform their various functions because they possess certain characteristics. These characteristics are described using the following terms: irritability, contractility, elasticity, and extensibility. Irritability refers to the ability of muscles to receive and react to stimuli from outside the body, such as the touch of massage, or to respond to internal stimuli, such as electrical currents sent from the brain. The muscle's irritability also refers to their reaction to heat, chemicals such as acids or salts, and other impulses. Contractility refers to muscles that are capable of shortening and therefore exerting force. An example of a muscle that possesses contractility is the cardiac muscle, which forces blood through the body as a result of the pumping action of the heart. Elasticity refers to the ability of a muscle to return to its original shape after being stretched. Extensibility is the ability of muscle to stretch beyond its original shape.

Skeletal muscles

Skeletal muscles are those which are striated and attached to the bones through tendons. When muscles constrict or expand, they exert a force on the tendon. The tendon pushes or pulls the bone, which causes the limb or appendage to move. Tendons are not as elastic as muscles, so the majority of the body's movement is due to muscles. Skeletal muscles are primarily voluntary. They do, however, possess some involuntary characteristics that can also cause the muscle to contract or expand. Massage focuses on a therapeutic regimen designed to enhance the function of muscles through techniques that bring about relaxation, release of toxins, greater flexibility, and a greater range of motion. All of these results are accomplished through specific, pressurized body movements.

Point of insertion

Muscles are connected by tendons that extend from either end of the muscle. In order for movement to occur, one side of the muscle, generally the part closest to the center of the body, is considered the point of origin. This area is not as flexible as the other end of the muscle because of the lack of space in the area, and also because a broader range of motion is not necessary for that area. At the other end of the muscle lies the insertion point. This area is more distal, and the majority of the movement takes place here. Both the origin and the insertion point of the muscle are attached to the bone by a tendon. When one knows the origin of the muscle, it is easy to infer which way the muscle will contract based on that knowledge.

Actions of muscles

Although muscles are distinct within the body, they work in conjunction with other muscles to perform actions. As such, the muscle performing the primary movement is known as the prime mover, or the agonist. To counteract this initial movement, a muscle on the opposite side causes an opposite reaction. This muscle is known as the antagonist. For example, a bicep that contracts would be the agonist, while a triceps that expands would be classified as the antagonist. It is important to understand the relationship between the muscles so an appropriate treatment plan that takes the movement of both muscles into consideration can be created. Any muscles that assist the prime mover are called synergists. A fixator is any muscle that helps to stabilize a body part so another muscle can move.

Major Muscles

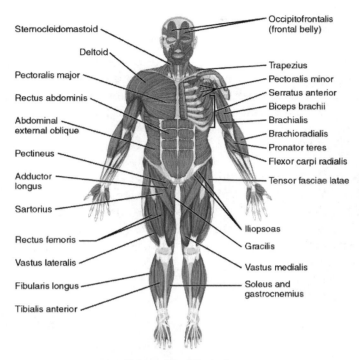

Sternocleidomastoid

Deltoid

Pectoralis major

Rectus abdominis

Abdominal external oblique

Pectineus

Adductor longus

Sartorius

Rectus femoris

Vastus lateralis

Fibularis longus

Tibialis anterior

Occipitofrontalis (frontal belly)

Trapezius

Pectoralis minor

Serratus anterior

Biceps brachii

Brachialis

Brachioradialis

Pronator teres

Flexor carpi radialis

Tensor fasciae latae

Iliopsoas

Gracilis

Vastus medialis

Soleus and gastrocnemius

Major muscles of the body.
Right side: superficial; left side:
deep (anterior view)

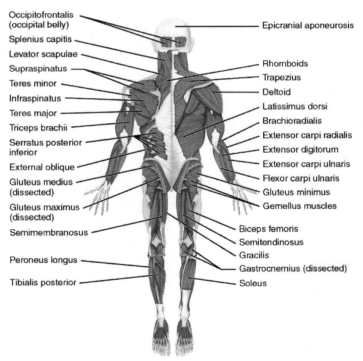

Occipitofrontalis (occipital belly)

Splenius capitis

Levator scapulae

Supraspinatus

Teres minor

Infraspinatus

Teres major

Triceps brachii

Serratus posterior inferior

External oblique

Gluteus medius (dissected)

Gluteus maximus (dissected)

Semimembranosus

Peroneus longus

Tibialis posterior

Epicranial aponeurosis

Rhomboids

Trapezius

Deltoid

Latissimus dorsi

Brachioradialis

Extensor carpi radialis

Extensor digitorum

Extensor carpi ulnaris

Flexor carpi ulnaris

Gluteus minimus

Gemellus muscles

Biceps femoris

Semitendinosus

Gracilis

Gastrocnemius (dissected)

Soleus

Major muscles of the body.
Right side: superficial; left side:
deep (posterior view)

Trapezius muscle

The scapula is located on the posterior upper region of the body and connects the arm bone to the collarbone. The scapula is also known as the shoulder blade, while the collarbone is referred to as the clavicle. The trapezius muscle is connected to the cervical spine from the occipital bone at the top of the spine down to the T5-T12 area of the lumbar column. Three types of trapezius muscles exist: upper, middle, and lower. Each corresponds to the region in which the muscles originate. These muscles are involved with the elevation, depression, and upward rotation of the scapula.

Rhomboid muscle

There are major and minor components of the rhomboid muscle. The rhomboid major can be found in the T2-T5 portion of the thoracic vertebral column. It is located deep within the trapezius muscle. The purpose of the rhomboid major is to keep the scapula in line with the ribcage. This muscle functions by pulling the scapula closer to the vertebral column. The rhomboid minor retracts the scapula downward. It is found between the C7-T1 vertebral column. Its point of insertion is at the base of the scapula.

Levator scapulae muscle

This muscle originates from the C1-4 vertebral column, which is located at the back and side of the neck. It helps to move the neck from side to side laterally. It inserts at the top third of the scapula.

Pectoralis minor muscle

This muscle originates between the 3rd and 5th ribs, close to the costal cartilage. The pectoralis minor draws the scapula downward and towards the thorax. It attaches to the coracoid process, which extends outward from the scapula.

Serratus anterior muscle

This muscle originates from anterior ribs 1-8 and causes an upward movement of the scapula. It provides stabilization and is also referred to as the "boxer's muscle" because it assists with protraction of the scapula.

Upper extremities muscle

Approximately eight separate muscles cause the upper arm to move. These muscles are listed below:
- Pectoralis Major (Clavicular and Sternal): helps to push the shoulder forward and rotate the arm towards the body
- Coracobrachialis: helps the arm swing forward
- Deltoid (Anterior, Middle, and Posterior): mainly responsible for lifting the arm away from the trunk at the shoulder
- Supraspinatus: primarily involved in abduction of the shoulder
- Infraspinatus: helps to extend the arm and rotate it to the outside
- Subscapularis: involved in the medial rotation of the arm

- Teres minor: involved with the adduction and lateral rotation of the arm
- Teres major: involved with arm extension and medial rotation
- Latissimus Dorsi: the major muscle of the upper back, which assists in moving the arm backward and rotating it inward

Pectoralis major and coracobrachialis muscles

The pectoralis major is divided into two groups: the clavicular portion and the sternal portion. The clavicular portion originates medially at the clavicle and inserts at the outer ridge of the bicipital groove. Its causative actions are the conduction of adduction, the moving of the limb closer to the body, medial rotation, and flexion of the humerus bone. The humerus is the long bone extending from the scapula at the shoulder to the radius and ulna at the elbow. The sternal portion of the pectoralis major originates from the sternum and the costal cartilage of ribs 1-6, but inserts at the outer ridge of the bicipital groove proximally. It acts on the arm in the same manner and also causes the extension of the humerus when it is flexed. The coracobrachialis originates at the coracoid process of the scapula (the portion of the scapula that extends frontward) and inserts at the middle of the humerus. It assists with the flexion and adduction of the humerus bone.

Deltoid muscle

The deltoid is a triangular-shaped muscle that provides the rounded shape to the human shoulder. It is divided into three sections: anterior, middle, and posterior. The main motion associated with the deltoid is the abduction of the arm. The anterior section originates at the outside third of the clavicle. It inserts at the deltoid tuberosity of the humerus and causes flexion and horizontal rotation of the humerus. The middle deltoid muscle originates at the acromion process of the scapula, and also inserts at the deltoid tuberosity. It assists with the adduction of the humerus to a 90-degree extension. The posterior deltoid originates at the lower part of the scapula and inserts at the deltoid tuberosity. It causes the extension, horizontal adduction, and lateral rotation of the humerus.

Supraspinatus muscle

This muscle originates at the supraspinous fossa of the scapula at the superior portion of this bone. Its insertion point is at the top of the humerus bone. This muscle acts upon the upper arm by instigating abduction in the humerus.

Infraspinatus muscle

This muscle originates at the infraspinous fossa of the scapula at the medial portion of this bone. It covers a much larger surface area than the supraspinous fossa. This muscle inserts at the greater tubercle, or large round nodule, of the humerus and assists in the lateral rotation of the humerus.

Subscapularis muscle

This muscle originates at the back surface of the scapula. This muscle inserts at the lesser tubercle of the humerus. Its function is to assist in the medial rotation of the humerus.

Teres major, teres minor, and latissimus dorsi muscles

The teres major is a thick, flat muscle located on the dorsal inferior side of the scapula. The insertion point is the lesser tubercle of the humerus. This muscle extends upward into the tubercle and is responsible for moving the humerus in a way that causes the arm to lower and move in a backward motion. The teres minor is a narrow, long muscle that is part of the rotator cuff. The insertion point is the lowest end of the greater tubercle of the humerus. It causes the humerus to move in a backward motion and also to rotate outward. The latissimus dorsi is a large, triangular, flat muscle located on the posterior side of the body. It covers the lumbar region and the last six of the thoracic vertebrae. This muscle extends upwards to insert at the intertubercular groove of the humerus. The actions it is responsible for are the extension, adduction, and internal rotation of the joint at the shoulder.

Biceps brachii muscle

The biceps brachii is the muscle located on the anterior upper arm. It is often referred to simply as the bicep. Its main purpose is to cause the flexion of the arm. The origin of the bicep is at the coracoid process of the scapula (short head) and the glenoid fossa (long head). It then extends down the arm and attaches at the radial tuberosity, a large nodule at the end of the radius. Because of the insertion point, the biceps brachii also influences the movement of the forearm.

Actions caused by the biceps brachii.

There are three actions caused by the biceps brachii: flexion of the forearm, extension of the arm above the shoulder joint, and the supination of the forearm (forearm rotation that results in the palms facing upwards). The triceps brachii is located on the posterior region of the upper arm. It originates at three points: the infraglenoid tuberosity of the scapula, the proximal half of the humerus, and the distal region of the humerus. The triceps brachii is responsible for extending the elbow. The biceps and triceps work in conjunction as flexors and extensors. The flexor contracts the muscle, causing the joint to bend, while the contraction of the extensor causes the limb to return to its original position.

Supinator muscle, pronator teres, and pronator quadratus

The supinator is a wide muscle that curves around the upper third of the radius. Its main purpose is to allow the hand and forearm to supinate, or twist, so that the palm of the hand either faces the body or faces forward. It also uses the bicep brachii muscle to perform this action. The supinator consists of two types of fibers: the superficial fibers and the upper fibers. This muscle can be difficult to palpate. The pronator teres and the pronator quadratus are two muscles that work together to pronate the hand so that the palm faces downwards towards the floor. The pronator teres originates at both the humerus and the ulna. It then attaches at the radius. The pronator quadratus runs from the distal part of the anterior ulna to the distal part of the anterior radius. This muscle assists not only with moving the palm to face downwards but also with keeping the bones of the radius and ulna together.

Flexion of the wrist

The muscles that play a part in causing flexion of the wrist are:
- Flexor Carpi Radialis – This muscle can be felt on the anterior side of the forearm. It can be palpated on the radial side of the palmaris longus tendon; it helps to flex and abduct the hand.
- Flexor Carpi Ulnaris (humeral head and ulnar head) – This muscle is located on the proximal half of the forearm; it helps to flex and adduct the hand.
- Palmaris Longus – This muscle originates from the humerus and inserts at the palmar aponeurosis, also known as the muscles of the palm of the hand. Somewhat superfluous, this muscle assumes a more prominent role when other muscles are injured.

Extension of the wrist

The muscles that play a role in causing the extension of the wrist are:
- Extensor Carpi Radialis Longus – This muscle originates at the distal third of the humerus and inserts at the base of 2nd metacarpal or index finger. It moves the wrist in such a way that the hand is moved away from the palm and towards the thumb.
- Extensor Carpi Radialis Brevis – This muscle originates on the lateral side of the humerus and inserts at the base of the 3rd metacarpal, or middle finger. It holds the wrist in place during flexion of the fingers and aids in the adduction of the hand.
- Extensor Carpi Ulnaris – This muscle originates on the lateral humerus and inserts at the lateral base of the 5th metacarpal, or pinky finger; it extends and adducts the wrist.

Finger Muscles

The following is a partial list of the muscles that act upon the fingers:
- Flexor Digitorum Superficialis: (includes humeral head, ulnar head, and radial head); flexes the wrist, interphalangeal joints, and hand
- Flexor Digitorum Profundus: flexes the distal and proximal interphalangeal joints, metacarpophalangeal joints (except the thumb), and the hand
- Flexor Digiti Minimi: flexes the little finger
- Extensor Digitorum: extends the wrist and the fingers (except the thumb)
- Extensor Indicis: extends the metacarpophalangeal joint of the index finger
- Extensor Digiti Minimi: helps to extend the wrist and the fifth metacarpophalangeal joint

Muscles that act upon the fingers
The following is a partial list of the muscles that act upon the fingers:
- Adductor Digiti Minimi: abducts and flexes the fifth metacarpophalangeal joint
- Opponens Digiti Minimi: coordinates the movements of the little finger in relation to the thumb
- Palmar Interosseous: (includes first, second, third, and fourth); helps to flex and adduct the metacarpophalangeal joints
- Dorsal Interosseous: adducts the 2nd and 4th metacarpophalangeal joints, assists in radial and ulnar deviation of the 3rd metacarpophalangeal joint, and flexes the 2nd, 3rd, and 4th metacarpophalangeal joints
- Lumbricals: flexes the metacarpophalangeal joints and extends the interphalangeal joints

Thigh and lateral rotators muscles

The muscles of the lateral rotators and thigh are made up of the gluteus maximus, which provides for lateral movement and support of the thigh; the gluteus medius, which adducts the thigh; and the gluteus minimus, which assists with rotating the hip. The internal rotators include the quadratus femoris, the obturator externus and internus, and the gemellus superior and inferior. These muscles aid in rotating the hip area. Additional muscle groups include the adductor brevis, the adductor longus, and the adductor magnus. These muscles assist with the extension and rotation of the thigh. The psoas major and the iliacus are located in the pelvic region and assist with flexing the thigh and hip and rotating the knee.

Upper leg muscles

The posterior thigh region is composed of the biceps femoris, the semi-tendinosis, and the semi-membranous. These muscles assist with extending the thigh and rotating the knee. The biceps femoris is more commonly known as the hamstring and is made up of the long head and the short head. The long head of the biceps femoris originates at the ischial tuberosity and the sacrotuberous ligament. It inserts on the lateral side of the fibula and the tibia. The short head originates at the lateral edge of the linea aspera, a rough ridge on the posterior portion of the fibula. Both of these help with the lateral rotation of the leg and hip. Other muscles that cause the leg to extend at the knee include the rectus femoris, vastus lateralis, vastus intermedius, and the vastus medialis.

Foot muscles

The following is a partial list of muscles that act on the foot and cause movement as a result of inversion, extension, and flexion:
- Popliteus: responsible for medial rotation and flexion of the leg below the knee
- Tibialis Anterior: responsible for dorsiflexion and inversion
- Peroneus Tertius: responsible for dorsiflexion and eversion; not present in all people
- Extensor Digitorum Longus: responsible for dorsiflexion and eversion of the foot as well as extension of the toes
- Extensor Hallucis Longus: responsible for dorsiflexion and inversion of the foot, as well as extension of the big toe

Muscles that act on the foot
The following is a partial list of muscles that act on the foot and cause movement as a result of inversion, extension, and flexion:
- Gastrocnemius (Medial Head and Lateral Head): responsible for flexing the knee during foot dorsiflexion and flexing the plantar during knee extension
- Plantaris: flexes the knee
- Soleus: responsible for plantar flexion
- Flexor Digitorum Longus: responsible for plantar flexion, inversion, and toe flexion
- Flexor Hallucis Longus: primarily responsible for plantar flexion, inversion, and toe flexion
- Tibialis Posterior: responsible for plantar flexion and inversion
- Peroneus Longus: responsible for eversion and plantar flexion
- Peroneus Brevis: responsible for eversion and plantar flexion

Abdominal region muscles

Several muscle groups act upon the abdominal area. These include the rectus abdominis, which is responsible for flexing the trunk and tensing the abdominal walls. The external obliques run alongside the external surfaces of the lower eight ribs. These muscles extend from below the armpit down towards the waist. They allow for bilateral movement and the side to side rotation of the trunk. The internal obliques lie just underneath the external and provide for the same movements as the external obliques. The transverse abdominis muscles lie underneath the rectus abdominis, and also help with flexion and compression of the abdominal wall. The rectus abdominis can be palpitated from the sternum down to the pubis. The external obliques can be felt on the lateral side of the abdomen. The internal obliques and the transverse abdominis are situated deep within the abdominal region; they cannot be palpitated.

Respiratory process muscles

The primary muscle used to assist with the respiratory process is the diaphragm. It is located between the upper lumbar vertebrae and within the region of the six lowest ribs and costal cartilage. The diaphragm has no insertion point. The main purpose of the diaphragm is to contract the muscles used for inspiration (the intake of air). The muscle cannot be palpitated but can be seen during the respiratory process. Other respiratory muscles include the intercostals, which are made up of the external, internal, and innermost components. These muscles are located between each of the ribs and serve to pull apart the ribs during inspiration, allowing for greater lung capacity. The serratus posterior superior, located near the collarbone, and the serratus posterior inferior, located at the base of the ribs, serve to expand the ribs outwards and downwards, which also leads to an increase in lung capacity.

Spinal column muscle

The following is a list of the muscles that run alongside the spinal column. All are difficult to palpitate through the skin.
- Quadratus Lumborum: responsible for lateral flexion of the spine
- Intertransversarii: located between the transverse processes of the vertebrae
- Interspinales: found in pairs located on either side of the contiguous vertebrae
- Rotatores: located only in the thoracic region; assists in flexion of the spine
- Multifidus: assists in the rotation of the spine
- Semispinalis: (includes capitis, cervicis, and thoracis); longitudinal muscles connected to the vertebrae
- Spinalis: (includes capitis, cervicis, and thoracis); bundled with a group of tendons and directly next to the spine
- Longissimus: (includes capitis, cervicis, and thoracis); help to extend the vertebral column, flex the spine laterally, and rotate the head and neck to either side

Muscles that aid in mastication

Mastication is defined as the act of chewing, which is the process by which the teeth break food down into smaller particles that are easily swallowed. Many muscles aid this process. The masseter is responsible for closing the jaw and can be found near the zygomatic arch and the mandible. The temporalis, which originates at the temporal bone, causes the jaw to close and retract. The buccinator, which originates at the maxilla and mandible, helps to keep the cheeks close to the teeth to allow the food to remain in place for chewing. The internal pterygoid helps to close the jaw and move the jaw from side to side. The external pterygoid causes the lower jaw to protrude forward, an action associated most often with an under bite.

Eye muscles

The muscles of the eye provide for side-to-side and up-and-down movement. They allow a person to focus on objects without moving their head. None of these muscles can be palpitated. The eye muscles are as follows:
- Levator Palpebrae Superioris – Causes the eyelid to open
- Superior Oblique – Causes the eye to turn out and downwards
- Superior Rectus – Causes the eye to rotate upwards
- Lateral Rectus – Causes lateral movement
- Inferior Rectus – Moves the eye downwards
- Medial Rectus – Moves the eye medially
- Inferior Oblique – Moves the eye upwards and out

Facial muscles

The muscles that are used to form the facial expressions associated with happiness, sadness, anger, etc. are aided by the following muscle groups:
- Epicranius: (also known as the occipitofrontalis); runs from the occipital bone to the frontal bone; helps to raise the eyebrow
- Corrugator: lowers the medial end of the eyebrow and wrinkles the brow
- Procerus: originates from the membrane that covers the bridge of the nose; assists the motion of the frontal bone
- Orbicularis Oculi: lowers the eyelids
- Nasalis: compresses the cartilage of the nose
- Dilator Naris: helps to manipulate the nostrils
- Quadratus Labii Superioris: raises the upper lip
- Zygomaticus: moves the mouth up and back
- Orbicularis Oris: puckers the lips
- Risorius: brings the edges of the mouth backwards; associated with a smile or grimace
- Depressor Anguli Oris: lowers the angle of the mouth
- Depressor Labii Inferioris: lowers the lower lip
- Mentalis: responsible for movement of the mouth back and down; associated with a frown
- Platysma: draws the lower lip down, wrinkling the neck and upper chest
- Auricularis: wiggles the ears

Forehead muscles

The muscle groups that assist the body to perform movements such as frowning, drawing the eyebrows together, wrinkling the forehead, and drawing the nose upwards are listed below:
- Epicranius (consisting of the occipitalis and frontalis) – This muscle originates just above the occipital ridge and inserts at the epicranial aponeurosis. This muscle draws the epicranius towards the back, or posterior, of the head. It also raises the eyebrows, which causes the forehead to wrinkle. This muscle is sometimes known as the occipitofrontalis.
- Corrugator – This muscle is also known as the corrugator supercilii. It is triangular in shape and is responsible for wrinkling the forehead and frowning.
- Procerus – The origin of this muscle is within the fascia over the cartilage in the nasal area. It inserts between the eyebrows and deep within the skin. This muscle is responsible for the action of wrinkling the nose.

Muscles that aid in the movement of the eyes and nostrils
The muscles that are involved with this region of the face include:
- Orbicularis Oculi – Controls the opening and closing of the eye. This muscle originates at the nasal bone and circles the eyeball. The insertion point of this muscle is all around the eye; the muscle blends in with the surrounding areas.
- Nasalis – This muscle originates above the incisors at the maxilla bone. It then blends in with the procerus muscle. The purposes of this muscle are to compress the bridge of the nostrils, allow the external area of the nostrils to elevate, or flare, and also to depress the tip of the nose.
- Dilator Naris – This muscle allows the nostril opening to expand. It originates at the greater alar cartridge and inserts at the end point of the nose.

Mouth muscles

There are about eight muscle groups that are responsible for the various movements of the mouth. They include:
- Quadratus Labii Superioris – This lies next to the nose and extends to the zygomatic arch. It is responsible for raising or elevating the upper lip.
- Zygomaticus (major and minor) – This muscle extends from one side of the zygomatic arch to the corner of the mouth. The contraction of this muscle causes the mouth to draw back and upwards; this movement is associated with smiling.
- Orbicularis Oris – This muscle originates from various muscles around the mouth and inserts at the lips. It is a circular muscle that allows the mouth to remain closed, aids in chewing, helps with speech, and aids in the formation of facial expressions.
- Risorius – This muscle originates over the masseter. It inserts at the muscle surrounding the mouth and at the corners of the mouth. It is responsible for moving the mouth backwards at an angle.
- Depressor Anguli Oris – This muscle is responsible for drawing the mouth into a downward position and is located at the outer edge of the chin.
- Depressor Labii Inferioris – This muscle helps to depress the lower lip.
- Mentalis – This muscle causes the chin to rise up and also enables a person to pout.
- Platysma – This muscle causes the mouth to move in a downward direction, enabling a person to form an expression of sadness. It also causes the skin of the neck to wrinkle.

Proprioception

Proprioception is the body's ability to gauge its own position in the external world. At all times, we are engaged in unconscious acts of proprioception that allow us to move around in harmony with our surroundings. Proprioception is often referred to as spatial orientation. Scientists believe that the human capacity for proprioception can be attributed to the endings of peripheral nerve fibers in the muscles and joints. The information that is obtained from these nerve endings is integrated with information from other sources, including the visual, auditory, tactile, and vestibular systems. The vestibular system senses the velocity of head movements and the relative pull of gravity on the body, and can, therefore, provide important information about the orientation of the body.

Muscle spasm

A muscle spasm is a dysfunction of the muscle in which involuntary contractions occur in a single muscle or a group of muscles. The intensity of these spasms can vary depending on the person's pain tolerance and how long the contractions continue. These spasms are classified as tonic when they remain in a contracted state for an extended time, and as clonic when the spasm relaxes between contractions. Another term for a muscle spasm is cramp. Typical kinds of spasms include hiccups, charley horses, twitches, and convulsions. Muscles can also spasm as a result of nearby injuries. When treating a spasm, massaging the area directly is not recommended until the acute spasm has subsided. It is thought that compressing the ends of the muscle or preventing the contraction of the antagonist muscles will help quiet the muscle spasm. Massaging the area after the acute phase has passed will help eliminate toxins from the muscle, introduce nutrients to the area, and restore circulation.

Muscle strains

The term muscle strains can also refer to torn or pulled muscles. There are generally three degrees of strains that can occur to the muscle. A grade 1 strain is when the muscle fibers have been overextended, but there are very few tears in the fibers. There is pain, but there are no visual marks on the surface of the skin. There is also no loss of muscle function. When a grade 2 strain occurs, there are partial tears in less than 50% of the muscle fibers. There is pain, tenderness, inflammation, and loss of function to some degree. A grade 3 strain is when more than 50% of the muscle fibers are torn. There is considerable pain, and the bleeding may be seen under the skin. Swelling and immediate loss of muscle function occurs. Recovering from these types of injuries usually involves the use of the R.I.C.E. method (rest, ice, compression, and elevation) and massage once the acute stage has passed. It is important to maintain a good range of motion and flexibility once this stage is over to prevent muscle atrophy and reduce scarring.

Hypertrophy and atrophy

It is possible for muscles to increase in size and get larger. As seen in bodybuilders, the size of the muscle increases through repeated strength training. This increase in the width of a muscle is known as hypertrophy. The muscular fibers themselves do not increase in number. Rather, the width of the muscle fibers increases. This increase causes the body part affected by the muscle to grow stronger. It will have more power while performing required actions or movements. Other changes that occur are an increase in the blood supply to the hypertrophic muscle and also an increase in ATP and mitochondria. Muscle atrophy refers to the degeneration and wasting away of muscles, which occurs as a result of disuse. Muscles that are not used break down and shrink, gradually losing their strength. The amount of blood supplied to the limb decreases, causing a change in the color of the limb. Atrophy commonly occurs in individuals with paralysis who have lost nerve connections to the muscles, which causes them to waste away.

Effects of diseases on muscular system

Tendonitis, tenosynovitis, and lupus

Tendonitis is the condition in which the tendon that connects the muscle to the bone becomes inflamed. Tenosynovitis is the inflammation that occurs along the tendon sheath. Both of these conditions cause pain, stiffness, and swelling of the affected area. Treatment regimens include massage over the inflamed area, the application of ice to decrease swelling, and physical manipulation to increase range of motion and assist with prevention of scar tissue. Lupus is an autoimmune disease that can affect tissues and organs. This disease affects the connective tissue and can cause pain throughout many areas of the body. With this disease, blood vessels may become inflamed and arthritis can occur. Massage therapy on a person with lupus should be performed under the supervision of a physician to prevent pain to the patient.

Fibromyalgia and muscular dystrophy

Fibromyalgia is a disease that also affects connective tissue, producing pain, stiffness, and fatigue in the muscles, tendons, and ligaments. Factors such as temperature, humidity, and infections can cause an increase in the person's discomfort level and trigger additional symptoms. With the pain levels of each person varying, it is important to work with the client's personal physician to develop a massage plan. Muscular dystrophy is a disease that causes progressive degeneration of the muscles in the body. The muscular fibers are gradually replaced by fat and connective tissues, eventually leaving the muscle unable to function. If it does not induce pain, massage is beneficial in preventing the onset of muscle degeneration.

Joints

The body has several different types of joint to allow for different kinds of movement. In a ball-and-socket joint, one of the connecting surfaces is rounded and the other is concave. As with all joints, a ball-and-socket joint is filled with fluid to allow for the smooth movement of the two parts. In a hinge joint, the convex surface of one joint fits against the concave surface of the other, and is arranged such that motion can only occur in one plane. An elbow is an example of a hinge joint. In a gliding joint, both connecting surfaces are basically flat, and so movement is very limited. The intercarpal joints connecting the mass of bones at the base of the hand is an example of a gliding joint.

Types of joints

In an ellipsoid joint, the oval-shaped section of one bone fits into the elliptical cavity of another. This connection allows for movement in two planes. The wrist is a classic example of an ellipsoid joint. In a pivot joint, a pointed or rounded area in one bone fits into a ring-like structure in another. In a joint like this, in the joint connecting the base of the spine and pelvis for example, the joint can only move by rotating. In a saddle joint, both of the connecting surfaces are shaped like saddles and fit together snugly. In this type of joint, movement can occur in two planes. The best example of a saddle joint is the one which connects the thumb to the hand.

Joint type	Example	Movement provided
Pivot	C1, C2 of neck	Rotation about an axis
Hinge	Elbow	Flexion and extension
Saddle	Carpal and metacarpal of the thumb	Flexion, extension, adduction, abduction, and circumduction
Gliding	Tarsal bones	Back and forth or side to side
Condyloid	Metacarpals and phalanges	Flexion, extension, abduction, adduction, and circumduction
Ball and socket	Hip	Flexion, extension, abduction, adduction, internal and external rotation

Joint capsules

A joint capsule is a sort of sleeve that surrounds a joint, preventing any loss of fluid and binding together the ends of the bones in the joint. The outside of this sleeve is made of a tough material, while the inside is softer and looser. In this way, movement is not impeded. Joint capsules are often especially stringy in areas where movement should be discouraged. For instance, there is a strong joint capsule section on the back of the knee, which is one reason why it is difficult for the lower leg to bend forward. The fibers of the outer joint capsule are known as ligaments; the inside of the joint capsule is called the synovial membrane. The synovial membrane secretes a fluid that keeps the joint lubricated and removes debris.

Ranges of motion

When describing the range of motion of a joint, massage therapists distinguish between the active, passive, and resistant ranges of motion. The active range of motion is the amount of flexibility the client is able to achieve without any external aid. The passive range of motion, on the other hand, is the degree of flexibility that can be achieved through the massage therapist's manipulations; no effort is expended by the client. Finally, the resistant range of motion is the degree of flexibility that can be achieved when the joint is acting against some form of resistance. For instance, a resistant range of motion assessment might measure the degree of flexibility of the elbow during a biceps curl.

Pathology, Contraindications, Areas of Caution, Special Populations

Common pathologies

The effects of massage therapy on many common pathologies are as follows:

- Asthma: tightening of the bronchial tubes; results in wheezing, coughing, and trouble breathing; massage can help to strengthen the muscles involved in breathing
- Chronic bronchitis: inflammation and infection of the bronchi; often occurs in conjunction with emphysema; massage can be helpful, so long as the patient is monitored closely
- Pneumonia: inflammation of the lungs; manifests as fever, chills, chest pain, cough, and difficulty breathing; massage is beneficial once the patient has passed out of the acute phase
- Cold: viral infection of the upper respiratory tract; symptoms can include fever, coughing, mucus overproduction, and headache; massage is helpful for managing symptoms and strengthening the immune system
- Atherosclerosis: hardening of the arteries; individuals with this condition should not receive rigorous circulatory massage
- Thrombus: a blood clot that remains fixed in the blood stream; massage is contraindicated
- Embolism: a blood clot that is moving through the bloodstream; massage is contraindicated
- Emphysema: hardening of the alveoli in the lungs; symptoms include trouble breathing, cough, and chronic respiratory infection; massage can be performed if the patient can breathe effectively and the condition is not acute
- Hypertension: high blood pressure in the pulmonary arteries; massage is indicated if the individual is not suffering from kidney or cardiovascular conditions
- Benign prostatic hyperplasia: irregular growth of the prostate gland; may cause problems with urination; does not prevent massage
- Endometriosis: overgrowth of endometrial cells in the peritoneal cavity; may lead to heavy menstruation, abdominal pain, and problems with intercourse and/or evacuation; massage is indicated, except in the affected area
- Peritonitis: inflammation of the membrane along the inner wall of the abdomen and pelvis; caused by infection or disease; manifests in severe abdominal pain; massage is contraindicated and the client should receive immediate medical attention
- Prostatitis: inflammation of the prostate gland; may result in chills, fever, testicular pain, pain in the lower back, and difficulty with urination; circulatory massage is contraindicated if the patient is in the acute phase
- Boils: bacterial infections on the skin; manifests as red sores; often appear in clusters; should not be massaged, especially because they may be quite contagious
- Bunions: a growth of the bone at the base of the big toe; should not be massaged
- Burns: may be first-degree (slight inflammation), second-degree (damage to epidermis), or third-degree (including damage to the dermis); once the burn has passed out of the acute stage, it may be massaged so long as it does not hurt
- Bedsores: lesions caused by impaired circulation; should not be massaged directly, although massage is a good way to prevent bedsores
- Fungal infections: manifest on the skin as red, itchy patches and blisters; may result in the weakening and infection of finger and toe nails; massage is contraindicated at the site of the infection

- Herpes: a virus that causes lesions and blisters; contraindicated in the acute stage and when the client has an infection or outbreak; equipment that comes into contact with the client should be washed
- Hives: a raised, scratchy patch of skin; usually caused by an allergic reaction; during the acute phase, massage is contraindicated everywhere; after the acute phase passes, massage is only contraindicated in the area of the hives
- Lice: parasitic insects; most often found on the scalp; symptoms include itching, irritation, and sores; massage is contraindicated, especially because lice are highly contagious
- Varicose veins: enlarged and twisted veins; may result in cramps and trouble with movement; massage is contraindicated locally
- Warts: small growths on the outer layer of skin; contracted by contact with another wart; massage is contraindicated locally
- Cysts: pockets of connective tissue surrounding a foreign body; should not be massaged directly
- Lyme disease: an inflammatory disease caused by a bacterium transmitted by deer ticks; can result in a rash, symptoms of influenza, and pain in the joints; massage can improve joint function during subacute phases
- Moles: pigmented spots on the skin; moles should not affect the delivery of massage services; however, moles that change in color or shape should be reported to the client's doctor
- Psoriasis: a red, scaly skin rash; most often located on the elbows, knees, and scalp; not contagious; contraindicated locally during the acute phase; indicated during the subacute phase
- Ulcers: any lesion that is eroding the membrane or surrounding skin; massage is contraindicated locally
- Tendinitis: inflammation of a tendon; usually caused by injury; massage is indicated, especially for reducing inflammation
- HIV/AIDS: a disease that ravages the immune system; HIV becomes AIDS when it integrates into the DNA of the individual; massage is indicated so long as the client is in relatively good health
- Cystic fibrosis: disease which results in exceptionally thick production of mucus, sweat, bile, and other body products; symptoms may include problems with breathing, coughing, and lung infections; massage is indicated, unless the patient's symptoms preclude it
- Cancer: a growth of malignant cells; massage can be beneficial so long as it does not reduce the body's strength during a period of intense and debilitating treatments
- Multiple sclerosis: a permanent disease; manifests in symptoms like numbness, blindness, and paralysis; massage is indicated in the subacute phase
- Depression: any diminution in quality of life, outlook, or happiness; massage can be extremely beneficial in mitigating the effects of depression
- Headaches: massage is indicated unless the headache is due to infection or damage to the central nervous system
- Premenstrual syndrome: a set of physical and psychological changes that occur directly before menstruation; symptoms can include breast tenderness, bloating, moodiness, and anger; bodywork can be especially beneficial while a woman is experiencing PMS
- Fever: slight increase in body temperature; massage is contraindicated; if a fever is greater than 102 degrees, the client should receive immediate physical attention
- Cerebral palsy: a family of injuries to the central nervous system; symptoms may include poor coordination, involuntary movements, and muscular disfiguration; massage can be very beneficial for individuals with cerebral palsy

- Meningitis: an inflammation of the membranes that surround the brain and spinal cord; can be caused by bacteria, protozoa, or viruses; massage is strictly contraindicated during the acute phase; once this passes massage can be beneficial
- Muscular dystrophy: a genetic disease in which the skeletal muscles gradually degenerate; may result in weakness, disability, and an inability to walk; massage can be quite effective at loosening muscles and improving circulation
- Bursitis: inflammation in the areas where tendons, ligaments, and bones come into contact; when acute, massage is contraindicated; otherwise, there is no restriction on massage
- Carpal tunnel syndrome: irritation of the nerves in the hands; often caused by repetitive tasks; massage may be beneficial, especially around the wrist area
- Encephalitis: swelling of the brain; caused by infection; symptoms include fever, headache, and disorientation; massage only contraindicated if the condition is acute
- Parkinson's disease: degenerative neurological disease; manifests in expressionless face, involuntary movements, tremor, and muscle weakness; massage is indicated, so long as the movements of the client are respected
- Heart attack: flow of blood through the heart is suddenly impeded; circulatory massage contraindicated during the recovery period
- Heart failure: heart is unable to supply enough blood to nourish the body; symptoms include lung fluid buildup, irregular pulse, and coughing; energetic massage is appropriate, but circulatory massage is strictly contraindicated
- Stroke: rapid death of brain cells; caused by a blockage of blood flow to the brain, which in turn results in an oxygen deficit; symptoms include loss of speech, weakness, and paralysis; all but the most vigorous circulatory massage is indicated for this group
- Gout: inflammation of the ankle and foot joints; feet and ankles will become swollen and painful; massage contraindicated
- Edema: build-up of fluid between the organs; manifests in bloated areas on the body; in a severe, "pitting" edema, the body will not return to its natural form when pressure is applied; massage is contraindicated
- Gallstones: crystals made of hardened bile or cholesterol; massage indicated unless the client is in severe pain
- Scarification: buildup of scar tissue, as for instance over a wound; massage is contraindicated during the acute period
- Pancreatitis: inflammation of the pancreas; often caused by alcoholism or gallstones; symptoms include abdominal pain, nausea, vomiting, and fever; massage is appropriate once the condition has been thoroughly treated by a doctor
- Hernia: small tear in the abdominal lining or inguinal ring; small intestine may poke through this hole; massage is contraindicated until the hernia has been treated
- Irritable bowel syndrome: an intestinal disorder in which the bowels and their nerves become over or under active; can manifest in abdominal pain, bloating, diarrhea, and constipation; massage is indicated; client should be monitored
- Tuberculosis: contagious infection; can only be identified by a chest x-ray.
- Hepatitis: viral infection of the liver; massage is contraindicated when the disease is acute
- Diabetes: disorders of the metabolism; manifests in problems with appetite, urination, and blood sugar balance; massage is indicated unless the patient has specific circulation problems
- Hemophilia: condition in which the blood fails to clot normally; vigorous massage is contraindicated, though gentle techniques may be beneficial

- Hypoglycemia: low blood sugar; can manifest in anxiety, palpitations, sweating, and nausea; this condition is episodic, so if an individual is experiencing a bout of hypoglycemia, he or she should receive treatment before a massage
- Lupus: a disease in which chronic inflammation leads to degeneration of the immune system; can manifest in diseases of the skin, heart, lungs, kidneys, joints, and nervous system; massage is indicated so long as the client is not experiencing an acute episode
- Herniated disc: the matter between the vertebral discs is forced out, which puts pressure on the spinal cord and nerves; massage is indicated, so long as the condition is not acute
- Fractures: cracked or broken bones; massage contraindicated in the area of the fracture, though it can be beneficial elsewhere
- Osteoarthritis: gradual inflammation, disintegration, and loss of the joint cartilage; most often affects the feet, hands, spine, hips, and knees; during acute inflammation, massage is strictly contraindicated
- Osteoporosis: reduction in bone mass; leads to a greater frequency of fracture; massage is indicated so long as the client is not in any great pain
- Urinary tract infection: infection of the kidney, ureter, bladder, or urethra; symptoms may include painful urination and abdominal pain; circulatory massage is contraindicated during the acute phase; massage in the lower abdomen is contraindicated during the subacute phase
- Hyperthyroidism: excessive thyroid hormone production; can result in high heart rate, weight loss, and depression; massage can be beneficial, as it can reduce stress
- Hypothyroidism: deficiency of thyroid hormone; can result in fatigue, constipation, and weight gain; massage is indicated if it does not aggravate any accompanying atherosclerosis
- Renal failure: failure of the kidneys; may result in jaundice, edema, and even death; massage is systemically contraindicated during the acute and chronic phases
- Influenza: virus of the respiratory tract; can result in fever, loss of appetite, and weakness; massage is only appropriate if the influenza has passed out of the acute phase
- Mononucleosis: a chronic infection; can last for one or two months; symptoms include fever, fatigue, sore throat, and swollen lymph nodes; massage is contraindicated during the acute phase
- Myasthenia gravis: an autoimmune neuromuscular disorder; manifests in extreme muscular fatigue; massage is indicated, though it will not improve the condition in any significant way
- Spina bifida: a birth defect in which part of the spine remains exposed; may result in incontinence, limited mobility, and learning difficulties; massage is indicated as part of a comprehensive physical therapy program
- Menopause: the end of a woman's menstrual periods; usually diagnosed when a woman has not menstruated for one year; some related symptoms include mood swings, hot flashes, and fatigue; massage is extremely useful during menopause
- Recovery from surgery: the client should receive permission from his or her physician before receiving massage treatment
- Hematoma: deep intramuscular bruising; may or may not be visible externally; massage is contraindicated for acute hematoma; sub-acute hematoma may benefit from gentle circulatory massage
- Tremor: unnatural, repetitive shaking of the body; may be caused by illness, medication, or fear; massage is indicated
- Plantar fasciitis: inflammation of the tissue that stretches from the heel to the ball of the foot; symptoms include pain and difficulty walking; massage is indicated, as it can delay the formation of scar tissue and improve circulation in the calves

- Shin splints: inflammation of the tibia; results from overuse; manifests in pain; massage is indicated so long as the client does not have a stress fracture
- Muscle spasms: short, involuntary muscle contractions; caused by stress, medication, and overuse; massage around the muscle connector sites can improve the condition and reduce painful symptoms

Herniated disk

A herniated disk is an invertebral disk that has protruded out and into the spinal cavity, causing pain and increased pressure on the spinal cord. This disk can also cause pain and radiating pressure on the nerve endings leading down the legs. Most often occurring in the lumbar region, the typical herniated disk occurs gradually over time. When seeing a physician for this condition, diagnostic tests may be ordered to determine the degree of severity. These tests can include x-ray, myelogram, CT scan, and MRI to determine the exact cause of the pain; the symptoms can mimic other illnesses or diseases. Initial treatment of a herniated disk includes hot or cold therapy, massage, exercise, stretching, rest, pain medication, and, in severe or prolonged cases, surgery.

Strain and sprain

Strains and sprains are two of the most common muscular injuries. They may be severe and painful, or so minor as to be almost unnoticeable. A strain is an injury that occurs when a muscle has been stretched beyond its capabilities. It can also be referred to as a pulled muscle. Microscopic tears in the muscle cause pain, stiffness, swelling, and sometimes bruising. A sprain is an injury that occurs when a ligament is overstretched suddenly, causing pain, immediate swelling, and bruising. Severe sprains involve a popping, either felt or heard, and loss of function of that body part.

Classifications of sprains
There are three main classifications of sprains. The first is identified as a class I sprain. This is when the ligament has been stretched, but there is little to no loss of limb function. The second is a class II sprain. The ligament is torn, and there is some loss of limb function. Some internal bleeding may occur, or there may not be any bruising or discoloration. The third type, a class III sprain, involves a complete tear of the ligament, along with internal bleeding and extensive loss of function of the affected limb. All three types of sprains heal best when the R.I.C.E. method (rest, ice, compression, and elevation) is used. Massage is recommended only during the latent stages of healing and will help prevent the formation of scars and increase range of motion and flexibility.

Infections

An infection within the body is an indication of the presence of microorganisms (such as bacteria, fungi, parasites, and viruses) that are capable of causing harm to the body. These microorganisms generally enter the body through cuts in the skin, through nasal passages, or by coming into contact with the bodily fluids of other individuals. The damage infections cause can range from simple, localized illnesses to diseases that ravage the entire body. Local infections are those that affect one small area of the body. If the infection has spread to other areas or all over the body, it is termed a systemic infection.

Inflammation

It is important that massage techniques are not performed on localized areas that are infected or, in cases of systemic infection, on any part of the body. Inflammation can result from an infection and causes five major changes to the body: redness, heat, swelling, pain, and loss of all or some function of the affected body part. Inflammation is an indicator of tissue damage. It is the result of an inflow of blood to the area and an increase in the production of white blood cells to aid in the healing process. It is important that these areas are not massaged while inflammation is present or while the patient has a fever.

Contraindications to massage

When performing a massage on a new client, it is important that the therapist obtain as thorough a medical history as possible. A contraindication is any procedure or treatment plan that, for the sake of the client's benefit and well-being, is not advisable. There are three types of contraindications that can exist: absolute, regional, or conditional. An absolute contraindication indicates that a massage should not be performed under any circumstances. Examples of this would include shock, pneumonia, and pregnancy-related toxemia. A regional contraindication exists when a client cannot have massage performed on a specific region of the body due to injuries, such as open wounds; contagious conditions that could cause harm to the therapist; or other conditions like arthritis. In the latter case, massage would result in additional pain to the client if the affected areas were massaged. The final type of contraindication is conditional. This means that the massage therapist must make accommodations in the therapeutic plan to help the client obtain the most benefit from the massage while avoiding the areas that could cause discomfort.

Massage on cancer patients

When performing a massage, the client's well-being is of the utmost importance. As such, the therapist should be aware of the contraindications of performing massage on a cancer patient.

A complete medical history should be taken, and the physician or oncologist should be consulted to determine if massage is a recommended and suitable form of treatment.
Factors to consider are:
- Location and type of cancer
- Stage of the cancer
- Additional sites for metastasis
- Treatment level of the cancer
- Immune system condition of the person at the time of the massage
- Stamina level and attitude of the person

During the actual massage, light or moderate pressure should be used. Areas where tumors are known to exist should not be subjected to deep massage.

Special Populations

Stress and pain during pregnancy

During a normal pregnancy, the mother can benefit from a massage, which will aid in decreasing the discomfort and aches associated with the back pain, leg pain, stress, and fatigue that occur during pregnancy. In order to provide the best care for the mother, it is important to note the mother's condition and to absolutely avoid massage when there is a risk of toxemia or pre-eclampsia. Massage is not an ideal way to address the high blood pressure, edema, nausea, and diarrhea associated with these conditions. Furthermore, massage can actually do harm to the mother. To prep the client, the massage therapist must ensure that both the mother and unborn child are in a comfortable position on the table, preferably facing up and in a semi-reclined position. If the client is lying on her side, it is important to place pillows under the head and between the knees to help support the back. Avoiding massage in the abdominal area is indicated. In addition, the therapist should not have the mother lie prone on her abdomen if she is in the latter stages of pregnancy.

Prenatal massage

While pregnancy is generally considered a happy time in a woman's life, it can bring about many physical changes that cause additional strain and stress on the body. These physical changes include a shifting of the joints to accommodate weight gain and the stretching of the ligaments to prepare the body for delivery. Some of these changes are due to hormones, and they can cause a pregnant woman to feel additional strain, which can only be relieved through rest and relaxation. The areas that are most often subjected to stresses during pregnancy include the neck, back, hips, legs, and feet. During massage, supporting cushions and bolsters can increase the comfort level of the mother and allow her to fully enjoy the benefits of massage. These benefits include inducing a relaxed state, improving the body's circulation, and soothing the nerves. The most common positions for the mother during massage include lying in the side-lying position and, during the earliest parts of the pregnancy, lying in the prone position.

Contraindications for prenatal massage

It is advised that massage therapy be performed in the prone position only during the first trimester, before the new mother is "showing." Reducing the time spent in this position helps to keep the fetus safe. At no time should prenatal massage be performed on the abdominal area. If the mother indicates problems with nausea, vomiting, diarrhea, or unusual vaginal discharge, massage should be withheld until the physician has been notified. In addition, if there is high blood pressure, lack of fetal movement, severe edema, or any abdominal pain, the mother should be referred to her physician immediately, as these symptoms can indicate a severe condition like toxemia or pre-eclampsia. A less serious condition to be aware of during prenatal massage would be the presence of varicose veins. Light effleurage may be performed in these areas, but moderate to heavy massage techniques should be avoided.

Infants

There is no reason why infants cannot receive as many positive benefits from massage as adults. There are some special considerations, however, when administering massage treatments to an infant. The duration of an infant massage is typically shorter, usually lasting about 15 minutes. Because infants cannot express themselves verbally, the massage therapist needs to be especially sensitive to signs of discomfort. It is best to use natural oil for lubrication. An infant massage usually starts with a client in the supine position. While in this position, the face, torso, arms, legs, and feet can be massaged. Effleurage, pétrissage, and tapotement can all be used during an infant massage. After a while, the infant can be placed into the prone position so that the back and neck can be massaged.

Elderly clients

Elderly individuals can receive many benefits from massage. Their skin and bones, however, may be more sensitive to stress and strain, so the massage therapist needs to be especially gentle when dealing with an elderly client. Also, elderly clients are more likely to be modest and may require more privacy when changing clothes. Elderly clients are likely to need special assistance while mounting and dismounting the massage table. Massage is contraindicated in elderly individuals with varicose veins, blood clots, or bedsores. At times, the improved circulation generated by massage therapy can confuse or disorient elderly clients, so the massage therapist needs to be especially sensitive to any signs of distress.

Disabled clients

Massage can be extremely beneficial for disabled individuals, so long as proper precautions are taken. Obviously, the precise precautions will depend on the disability. Individuals with sensory impairment, deafness or blindness for example, can receive normal massage therapy, though the therapist needs to be especially careful to clearly explain the success of the elements of the treatment. Clients who are on crutches are likely to have excessive strain on their triceps and wrists, while clients using wheelchairs are likely to have excessive tension in the muscles of the upper arm and back. When dealing with a paralyzed client, be sure to use gentle pressure, as the client will not be able to indicate injurious amounts of stress.

Pharmacology

Pharmacology is the study of the effects that drugs have on living organisms. With a large number of individuals on prescription therapy, it may be common for the massage practitioner to encounter someone who is on drug therapy, but also needs the services of a massage therapist. Medications can cause side effects that, if not made known to the massage practitioner, will continue in spite of treatment. As an example, some medications cause muscle pain and weakness. When the therapist is knowledgeable about the types of medications a client is taking, he or she can then adapt the massage sessions to avoid certain areas. Additionally, some medications may provide the same benefits as those obtained by massage. In these cases, the individual may see a decreased need for medication due to the relief obtained through massage. Part of the initial consultation should involve taking an inventory of the medications, supplements, vitamins, and herbs the client is taking.

Anti-anxiety drugs

Anti-anxiety drugs influence the central nervous system and calm an individual's violent reaction to stress. There are two classes of anti-anxiety drugs:
- Benzodiazepines: act by reducing the activity of the neurons in the brain; common brands include Halcion, Valium, Xanax, and Ativan; during massage, the client is at risk of entering a deep parasympathetic state, and should be monitored for dizziness
- Buspirone HCl: acts by reducing the uptake of dopamine and serotonin in the brain; sold under the brand name BuSpar; the client should receive extra stimulation during massage, as the nervous system may be suppressed

Antidepressants

Antidepressant medications alter the chemistry of the brain in order to alleviate the symptoms of depression. These drugs often take up to a month of use before yielding any positive results. There are three major classes of antidepressants, along with some other miscellaneous medications:
- Tricyclics: act by influencing the production of norepinephrine, serotonin, and acetylcholine; common brands include Tofranil, Elavil, and Norpramin; may result in dizziness during massage
- Monoamine oxidase inhibitors: act by limiting the activity of monoamine oxidase; common brands include Marplan and Nardate; sleepiness and dizziness may result from massage
- Selective serotonin reuptake inhibitors: act by managing the neurotransmitter serotonin; common brands include Prozac, Zoloft, Lexapro, Paxil, and Celexa; massage can occasionally lead to nausea or abdominal pain
- Miscellaneous anti-depressants: common brands include Effexor, Wellbutrin, and Serzone

Anti-inflammatories and analgesics

These medications are typically prescribed for individuals suffering from muscle pain. For this reason, massage therapists should be careful not to unwittingly injure a patient whose pain threshold is lower than normal. There are five classes of anti-inflammatories and analgesics:

- Salicylates: reduce fever and sensitivity to pain; common brands include Aspirin and Doan's Aspirin; vigorous massage should be avoided
- Acetaminophen: reduces pain and fever, but does not reduce inflammation; may be combined with caffeine or barbiturates; common brands include Tylenol and Anacin; massage should be gentle
- Nonsteroidal anti-inflammatory drugs: reduce inflammation and pain; common brands include Celebrex, Advil, Excedrin, Nuprin, and Aleve; watch out for abdominal bleeding and nausea
- Steroidal anti-inflammatory drugs: reduce inflammation, pain, and edema; common brands include Cortisone, Prednisol, and Decadron; deep-tissue massage should not be performed on clients who have been taking these drugs for a long time
- Opioids, mixed opioids: common brands include Codeine, OxyContin, Percocet, Darvon, Vicodin, and Demerol; morphine is also an opioid; massage should not include deep-tissue work, and the therapist should monitor the client's responsiveness

Autonomic nervous system disorder medications

These drugs are designed to treat conditions affecting the sympathetic and parasympathetic nervous systems. There are four classes of autonomic nervous system disorder medications:

- Cholinergics: act in a manner similar to the parasympathetic nervous system; common brands include Urecholine and Carbastat; massage should be gentle and the client should be monitored for responsiveness
- Anticholinergics: these drugs either stimulate or suppress particular organs or parts of the nervous system; common brands include Atropine, Ditropan, and Anaspaz; massage should be performed with the particular action of the drug taken into consideration
- Adrenergic drugs: act by stimulating the sympathetic nervous system; common brands include Dopamine, Epinephrine, and Albuterol; it may take longer to induce a parasympathetic response from a client taking this kind of medication
- Adrenergic blockers: hinder the action of the sympathetic nervous system; common brands include Flomax, Migranal, and Cardura; it will be easy for the client to enter a deep parasympathetic state

Cardiovascular drugs

Calcium channel blockers, and ACE inhibitors

Cardiovascular drugs either expand blood vessels or decrease the response of the sympathetic nervous system, thereby reducing the amount of stress placed on the heart. There are seven major classes of cardiovascular drugs:

- Beta blockers: act by reducing the impact of the sympathetic nervous system on the heart; common brands include Inderal, Normodyne, and Levatol; blood pressure should be monitored during massage
- Calcium channel blockers: expand the blood vessels; common brands include Norvasc, Cardene, and Isoptin; clients may suffer from dizziness, low blood pressure, and flushing
- ACE inhibitors: increase evacuation of water and sodium; common brands include Lotensin, Captopril, and Vasotec; may result in extremely low blood pressure

Digitalis, antilipemic drugs, diuretics, and antianginal medication

- Digitalis: strengthens and improves the efficiency of the heart; common brands include Digitek and Lanoxin; circulatory massage should be avoided
- Antilipemic drugs: reduce the amount of cholesterol in the blood; common brands include Questran, Lopid, Zocor, and Crestor; constipation and cramping are two common concerns that should be considered before the initiation of massage therapy
- Diuretics: increases the amount of urine created by the kidneys; common brands include Lasix, Bumex, Thalitone, and Lozol; care should be taken to avoid stressing the kidneys or reducing the blood pressure to a dangerous level
- Antianginal medications: either increase the amount of oxygen sent to the heart or reduce the heart's need for oxygen; common brands include Cedocard, Monoket, Nitrostat, and Nitro-Glycerin; the massage should be stopped immediately if hypotension, dizziness, or cramping occur

Cancer drugs

Cancer drugs are administered to kill or stop the production of cancer cells. Remember that these drugs act by more or less attacking all the cells of the body, and clients will, therefore, be severely debilitated. For this reason, extreme care should be taken during massage therapy. There are six major classes of cancer drugs:

- Alkylating drugs: common types include nitrogen mustards, ethylamines, alkyl sulfonates, triazenes, piperazines, and nitrosoureas
- Antimetabolite drugs: common brands include Cladribine, Aminopterin, and Cytarabine
- Antineoplastics: can be antibiotic, hormonal, natural, or other; these drugs inhibit the growth and development of malignant cells

Clot management drugs

Clot management drugs manage the body's ability to stop bleeding. In a normal body, blood clots are formed from a combination of red blood cells, white blood cells, and platelets. There are two classes of clot management drugs:
- Anticoagulants: encourage the liver to produce chemicals that limit the formation of new blood clots; common brands include Heparin and Lovenox; clients on this medication may be susceptible to bruising
- Antiplatelet drugs: act by preventing platelets in the blood from congregating at potential clot sites; common brands include Aspirin, Pletal, and Empirin; clients may be especially susceptible to bruising

Diabetes management drugs

The number of people taking diabetes management medications is steadily increasing in the United States. A massage therapist must monitor the client closely during massage, as a sudden decrease in blood glucose levels has the potential to induce a hypoglycemic episode. There are two classes of diabetes management drugs:
- Insulin: enables the body to obtain energy from glucose in the blood; common brands include Humulin, Lantus, and Novolin; the injection area should be avoided during massage, and, if possible, clients should receive massage towards the beginning of their insulin cycle
- Oral glucose management drugs: reduce the production of sugar in the liver and increase the production of insulin in the pancreas; common brands include Diabinese, Glucotrol, Lucophage, and Precose; clients are at an increased risk of experiencing a hypoglycemic episode when taking this kind of medication

Muscle relaxants

Muscle relaxants reduce the amount of tension in muscular tissue. For this reason, it is especially important for massage therapists to be restrained in the amount of force they use during bodywork. These drugs are primarily prescribed to alleviate muscle spasms and the resulting pain. There are two classes of muscle relaxants:
- Centrally-acting skeletal muscle relaxants: act by depressing the central nervous system; common brands include Soma, Paraflex, Valium, Norflex, and Flexeril.
- Peripherally-acting skeletal muscle relaxants: act by diminishing the contractions of the muscles; commonly sold under the brand name Dantrium; stretching should not exceed the client's normal range of motion during massage.

Thyroid supplement drugs

Thyroid supplement medications are prescribed to treat hypothyroidism. There are three classes of thyroid supplement drugs:
- Levothyroxine sodium: imitate the natural secretions of the thyroid; common brands include Synthroid, Eltroxin, and Levoxyl; massage is indicated, and should not react with medications in any adverse way
- Desiccated extract: imitate the actions of the hormones produced by a healthy thyroid; common brands include Armour Thyroid, Nature-Thyroid, and Westhroid; no real effect on massage
- Liothyronine sodium: these drugs fulfill the same functions as other thyroid supplements and are generally only prescribed when the others are ineffective; common brands include Cytomel and Triostat; no negative interaction with massage

Definition of drug

Drugs are any chemical or herbal substances that are used to relieve the symptoms of an illness or disease. The term "drug" can also be used to refer to illegal substances that alter the mind's perception and the body's movement. Oftentimes, the drugs prescribed by a physician can produce adverse side effects on the human body that can interfere with any benefits obtained the drug. Some drugs have the ability to affect an entire system of the body, including drugs that affect the circulatory system. Some other drugs cause only a localized reaction, such as those used to alleviate the pain of a broken leg.

Classifying drugs

The federal Food and Drug Administration classifies drugs in order to protect the safety of the consumer. Drugs do not affect all individuals in the same manner, as a person's age, body weight, and height help to determine how fast the body absorbs the drug. Drugs are given a generic name when they are created by a pharmaceutical company. A specific trade name is then given to help consumers identify it and make it easier to remember. Drugs are classified according to their therapeutic abilities; thus, the same drug can fall under more than one classification.

Herbal supplements and vitamins

Herbal remedies have been around for many years, and their origins can be traced back to many cultural groups, including Native American and Chinese societies. Herbs have many uses, from cooking to decoration and to healing. Depending on the purpose of the plant and the need for it, all parts may be used, from the flowers and seeds down to the roots. Compared to chemically-based drugs, herbs are more commonly prescribed by physicians in other parts of the world. Approximately 25% of all prescription drugs come from a natural botanical source, unlike other drugs that are chemically manufactured in a lab environment. People tend to purchase herbs and supplements as a means of preventing disease and maintaining good health, and as an additional form of treatment that is used in conjunction with standard pharmaceutical treatment methods. The massage therapist should have an understanding of the effects of herbal supplements because of their widespread use and because their effects could interact with prescription medications.

Benefits and Physiological Effects of Techniques that Manipulate Soft Tissue

Physiological Effects of Soft Tissue Manipulation

Western massage, otherwise known as Swedish massage, helps to relax the body, increase metabolism, speed healing, and provide emotional and physical relaxation. Similar massages on two individuals can produce two entirely different reactions. Techniques used in Swedish massage include light touches and gentle stimulation over the skin, which produce reflexive sensations. Mechanically stimulating the body by increasing pressure on the muscles and tissues results in an increase in blood flow to the area, causing an increase in nutrients and oxygen as well as the removal of wastes from the muscle. By the end of the massage session, the body is in a more relaxed state. There is an increase in flexibility and a decrease in pain. An increase in the production of sweat and oil from the glands can be seen by the end of the massage. There is an improvement in blood flow to the area, resulting in a temporary color change in the skin. Finally, the temperature of the skin increases.

Effects on muscular structure

When a massage is being performed, the muscles undergo a transformation that helps them increase their nutritional intake, improves circulation, and helps to stimulate cellular activity within the muscle. Massage relaxes tense muscles and helps to alleviate the pain associated with muscle spasms. During a massage, blood passes through the muscular tissue at a rate that is three times greater than when the muscle is at rest. This action brings new supplies of blood to the area and assists with the removal of waste material. After strenuous exercise, massage helps to alleviate the pain, stiffness, and soreness associated with the exercise. If massage is prescribed as a therapy after an injury, there is less scarring and buildup of connective tissue in the muscles. Range of motion is also increased through massage. Circulation is also increased, which helps to reduce the time lost due to the injury.

Effects on nervous system

The nervous system is comprised of the central nervous system (made up of the brain and spinal cord) and the peripheral nervous system (made up of the autonomic nervous system, cranial nerves, and spinal nerves). The nervous system has the ability to be either stimulated or soothed, depending on the type of muscle massage being utilized. Techniques that stimulate the body include friction, percussion, and vibration. Light rubbing, rolling or wringing of the skin is known as the technique of friction. Percussion involves a series of tapping to increase the nervous irritability. Depending on the duration, percussion has the ability to numb the nerves within the area. Vibration involves applying shaking or trembling movements on the body part. The end result is the stimulation of peripheral nerves. Soothing techniques that produce a calming effect include light stroking of the skin and pétrissage, which are light, kneading movements on the skin. Putting pressure on a specific trigger point desensitizes the area and releases hypertension in the muscle.

Effects on autonomic nervous system

The autonomic nervous system is divided into two distinct areas: the sympathetic nervous system and the parasympathetic nervous system. The sympathetic nervous system is responsible for the "fight or flight" response, while the parasympathetic system counters these effects and helps to return the body to a relaxed state by reducing the heart rate and increasing circulation to bring about a relaxed state of being. The sympathetic nervous system, by contrast, increases the alertness of the body through the release of adrenaline and epinephrine. When a massage is performed, the reaction from the autonomic nervous system is initially one of invigoration, which gradually mellows into relaxation and sedation. The parasympathetic nervous system is stimulated, leading to a reduction in epinephrine, norepinephrine, and blood pressure.

Effects on circulatory system

When techniques such as massage, pressure, stroking, and percussion are performed on the body, the circulatory system responds in a favorable manner, which benefits the entire body. Stroking the skin lightly causes dilation in the capillaries. Applying stronger pressure while stroking leads to the skin taking on a flushed look and a longer-lasting period of dilation. Percussion of the muscles causes the blood vessels to contract; they gradually ease up and cause a relaxed state. Applying friction to the muscles and skin rapidly produces a response, in this case, the flow of blood through the veins. It also accounts for the flow of interstitial fluid, which leads to a healthy cellular environment. Kneading the muscles causes the blood to flow into the deeper sections of arteries and veins. Lighter massage techniques are responsible for lymph circulation, as they diminish the tendency towards edema in these areas. Compression causes muscles to store a larger quantity of blood. Finally, all massage techniques should be directed towards the heart: from the ends of the appendages towards the torso and also from the head downward.

Pain relief

The massage therapist should pay close attention to areas of concern in the patient's body before, during, and after the massage. Techniques used during the massage have the ability to alleviate any suffering caused by pain or stress. Of particular interest to the therapist are methods that can relieve the pain of a pain-spasm-pain cycle, which is indicated by ischemia (decreased blood flow to the area within a muscle). A proper therapeutic massage increases blood flow to an area, creating pleasurable sensations where there was previously only marked pain. The nerve endings carry these signals to the brain, causing the overall feeling of calmness and relaxation throughout the body. To combat ischemia, the massage therapist should focus on breaking the pain-spasm-pain cycle and increasing mobility in that area. Through therapeutic palpations, the exact area of pain can be identified. The therapist can then focus the massage in that area, reduce the amount of lactic acid within the muscle, and introduce oxygen and other nutrients to help speed healing.

Pain management

Pain management is one of the benefits obtained through massage therapy, as the muscle receives an influx of blood circulating through the tissue. Through a process known as gate control theory, the transmission of pain sensations from the affected area is interrupted and prevented from reaching the central nervous system. This is accomplished through stimulating the cutaneous receptors. Massage techniques such as rubbing and applying pressure also prevent the pain sensation from reaching the receptors in the brain. An example of this response is the reduction in the degree of pain that results from rubbing an area that has been struck.

Stress

When a person experiences significant stress in his or her life, it causes physiological and psychological changes in the body. At the physiological level, heart rates can increase, adrenaline rises, sweating may occur, and tightness can be felt within the muscles of the body as the skin prepares for a "fight or flight" response. Psychologically, a person may feel overwhelmed, depressed, moody, or sad, and may even take drastic measures to deal with the stress, such as consuming alcohol or using drugs. Massage is indicated as a means to help alleviate negative stress through the personal human contact inherent in treatment, and through ridding the body of toxins and waste in the cells. During the initial massage therapy consultation, the practitioner should be aware of any indicators of extreme stress and outline a plan that will bring relaxation to the client in a timely manner. At no point should the practitioner assume the role of a psychotherapist or counselor.

Differentiation between pain and stress

Pain causes sensations that range from slight to severe. It indicates potential damage to the tissues or possible destruction within the body. Pain can be an indication of damage to nerve endings that lie beneath the surface of the skin, damage to the periosteum of the bones, damage to blood vessels and arteries, and finally, deeper damage to internal organs and muscles. The body's response to pain is both physical and physiological, which means that the body's response to pain mimics the reaction that the body has to stress. Stress is any condition that causes strain on the body or tension within the body. It can affect the internal balance and harmony within the body. Stress affects each person differently at varying levels. Overall, increased stress can be detrimental to the health of the individual. The body's reactions to stress include an increased heart rate, the secretion of "fight or flight" hormones from the adrenal gland, deeper breathing, and increased blood pressure.

Dopamine and serotonin

During a massage, some of the chemicals released within the body produce positive physiological effects. Neurotransmitters such as dopamine and serotonin are released, which contribute to pain control and mood elevation. One neurotransmitter is dopamine, which helps to control the brain's emotions, motor skills, and feelings of pleasure or pain. Serotonin is another type of neurotransmitter that also helps regulate moods, behavior, appetite, and memory. Low levels of serotonin can contribute to depression, anxiety, sleep disorders, and even personality disorders. Massage helps to increase the levels of these neurotransmitters within the body and leads to a sense of peacefulness and calmness that can help reduce stress. Massage also contributes to appetite control and increased function of the immune system.

Therapeutic massage and anatomy and physiology

Therapeutic massage is defined as the process of applying techniques such as effleurage, pétrissage, stretching, and stroking on the muscular structure of the body to ease pains in the tendons, ligaments, muscles, and surface of the skin. This type of massage is intended to create a sense of calmness and relaxation, as well as to alleviate any pain, stiffness, or soreness in the body. Increased circulation, greater flexibility, improved muscle tone, and improved posture are additional effects that therapeutic massage has on the body. Having a basic understanding of human anatomy allows the massage therapist to focus on the parts of the body that require additional consideration and enables him to avoid measures that can cause pain to the client.

Physiological changes include the lowering of the client's blood pressure, reduction in the heart rate, and slower, deeper breathing, all of which contribute to the relaxed state of the client.

Massage movements

The basic massage movements are as follows:
- Touch – includes superficial and deep massage
- Gliding or effleurage movements – moving the hand or forearm over the body while applying varying amounts of pressure; can be aura stroking, superficial, or deep
- Kneading – includes pétrissage, rolling, lifting, and squeezing of the skin
- Friction – causing one layer of skin tissue to rub against another; can be performed by rolling, compressing, wringing, and vibrating
- Percussion – alternately striking the surface of the skin through cupping, slapping, tapping, and beating
- Joint movements – manipulating the limbs of the body through passive or active movements

Touch

Touch is defined as the action of initiating skin-to-skin contact between the massage therapist's hand and the client's body. Touch does not involve any movement. The pressure can range from extremely light to deep pressure, depending on the type of reaction the therapist is trying to achieve. Touch can have a calming physiological effect on the client. The massage therapist should open the massage session with a few moments of touch as a means of connecting with the client and becoming comfortable with his personal body space. This gentle touching is also performed at the end of the massage to signal the end of the session and provide a sense of closure for both the client and the therapist. Deep pressure can also be applied through touch. In this sense, touch is applied to calm, anesthetize, or stimulate the muscles. It is often used to soothe muscle spasms or alleviate pain. Force is applied through body movements rather than by relying only on the strength of the therapist's arms.

Techniques

Gliding Techniques

Ethereal stroking and feather stroking

The types of movements that are based on maneuvering the hand over the client's body with varying degrees of pressure are known as gliding techniques. Ethereal or aura stroking is the process in which the practitioner glides his hands over the length of the client's body, but does not actually touch the body. The intention of this practice, according to some philosophies, is to smooth over the energy field that surrounds the body. A second type of gliding technique is feather stroking, which involves making long, gentle strokes from the center of the body outward.

Effleurage and deep gliding

Effleurage is a common Swedish massage technique that calls for successive strokes over a long surface of the body. The pressure is increased with each stroke. Superficial gliding involves applying light pressure to the body with the hand over all surfaces. This gives the therapist a chance to assess the condition of the muscles prior to commencing the massage. The amount of pressure exerted, the part of the hand that is used, and the way that the pressure is applied must all be considered when the deep gliding technique is being performed. Deep gliding strokes are designed to stretch and broaden the muscle tissue and fascia. It is best to make these movements towards the heart to encourage blood and lymph flow.

Pétrissage

Kneading, or pétrissage, is used on the fleshy parts of the body to bring about the movement of fluid in deep tissues and help stretch the muscle tissue. The skin is generally raised between the hands and kneaded with firm pressure in circular motions. Often, both hands are used to perform this motion. In the type of pétrissage known as fulling, the tissue is lifted up and then spread out to enhance the area in between the muscular tissue. Another form of pétrissage is called skin rolling. In this method, the fingers pick up the skin in alternate motions and gently pull it away from the underlying tissues to create a stretching of the fascia. This motion warms the skin and helps to remove any buildup of adhesions on the tissue.

Circular and cross-fiber friction

Friction helps to move the superficial layers of tissue against the deeper tissues within the body. The action of applying friction creates warmth when the therapist presses tissue upon tissue, thereby flattening it, releasing fluids from the tissue, and also stretching it at the same time. The warmth produced also causes the client's metabolic rate to increase. Types of friction methods include circular friction and cross-fiber friction. As the name implies, circular friction involves moving the fingers or hands over the client's skin in a circular pattern. Cross-fiber friction is performed in a sharp, transverse direction to the muscle being worked on. This is the preferred method used when a specific muscle group is being rehabilitated; it promotes the rebuilding of elastic tissue fibers.

Percussion techniques

Slapping and tapping

Percussion movements are quick, striking motions that are made alternately against the body. This technique serves to stimulate the body. The movements do not involve the application of great force. The types of percussion movements are slapping, tapping, cupping, hacking, and beating. Slapping involves applying pressure from the flat palm of the hand against the surface of the body. Tapping involves using the fingertips in such a way that only the pads of the fingers come in contact with the body. The fingers can be either held in a flexed position or straight. Either way, the pressure applied is very light.

Cupping, hacking, and beating

Cupping involves shaping the hand into a curved shape prior to applying it to the body. This method is generally used on the rib area and is a technique commonly used by respiratory therapists to eliminate build up and congestion in the lungs. Hacking is the use of the ulnar side of the hands to strike the body, which causes an improvement in circulation and relaxation. Beating involves using loose fists to gently pound the body and is considered the heaviest and deepest form of percussion. This technique is used primarily on the dense muscle tissues.

PJM

One type of joint movement is known as passive joint movement (PJM). It is generally performed when the client is in a relaxed state and the therapist is able to maneuver, exercise, and stretch a part of the body. PJM is also used to determine the extent of any injuries to the client and to determine the exact range of motion that part of the body can achieve. Working the muscle and joint in this way allows the therapist to help improve the mobility of the joint and extend its range of motion. To perform the passive joint movement, the therapist must take care to move the limb only in the direction that it is designed to move, without any forceful or sharp gestures. If the movement is being done to assess damage, stopping at the point of the client's pain is indicated. To rehabilitate the joint, further extension of the limb is recommended.

AJM

In active joint movement (AJM), the client is responsible for contracting the muscle to perform the required movement of the joint. It is commonly used as an assessment tool to determine the exact capabilities and the range of motion of the client. The results can be benchmarked at the start of treatment, with a comparison made at the end of treatment to note the progress made. Active assistive joint movement is performed when the client attempts to move the joint through a series of movements. The therapist assists when the client no longer has the strength or ability to move the injured limb further. This is primarily a therapeutic device designed to restore mobility in the limb. Another type of joint movement is active resistive joint movement. In this action, the therapist or practitioner applies resistive force against the motion of the limb. This allows for the buildup of muscle strength that, in turn, leads to increased use of the limb. Resistive motions such as these can be applied to any body part.

Heat applications

Massage therapists use a number of heat applications to stimulate circulation and alleviate tissue soreness. For the most part, heat applications involve moist heat in the form of hot baths and hot towels. At all times, a massage therapist needs to be careful not to burn the client or raise the body temperature excessively. These days, massage therapists typically use silica gel packs, which can be reused between clients. Hot applications should never be placed under the body and should not cover more than 1/5 of the surface area of the body so that they do not affect body temperature. In general, hot applications are best used on specific, localized areas, such as when a client is experiencing tension or stiffness in a particular part of the body.

Cold applications

Massage therapists use cold applications to reduce body temperature, diminish circulation, and numb a particular area of the body. Cold applications may take the form of compresses (cold, wet cloths) or direct applications of ice. Applying ice to a particular part of the body for 10 minutes can reduce a client's sensitivity to pain a great deal. Ice also diminishes inflammation. Inflammation should only be treated with the ice when the massage therapist is certain of its origin. At no time should more than 1/5 of the client's body be subjected to a cold application, as this can dangerously affect body temperature. When the cold application is being used, the massage therapist should remove it every two or three minutes to make sure the skin is not blistering.

Important terms

Compression is the rhythmic movement of the hands or fingers on the muscular tissue. Palmar compression is directed onto the muscles transverse from the bone. It does not require the use of oils or lotions and, in fact, can be performed over clothing. It is commonly used in sports massage.

Rolling is the method in which a body part is rapidly passed back and forth between the hands. This results in warmth and encourages relaxation of the deeper muscle tissue.

Chucking is the process by which the tissue is grabbed between the hands and moved up and down along the length of the bone. This method is performed rather quickly.

Wringing is a process that is similar to wringing water from a towel. The hands move in opposing directions as the flesh is twisted against the bone.

Vibration is a movement that is performed either manually or in conjunction with a device that produces continuous trembling movements against the muscle. This action helps to desensitize and numb the area.

End feel – This occurs when the practitioner moves a client's joint through the range of motion and, just before the end point, feels a change in the quality of the movement. This sense of resistance, whether attributable to physiologic or anatomic factors, is known as the end feel.

Hard end feel – This is the feeling of bone rubbing against bone. A common location where this occurs is in the elbow joint.

Soft end feel – This is the limitation that occurs when moving a joint due to the location of soft tissue, which prevents additional movement.

Empty end feel – This is the presence of pain when moving a joint, which ends up causing restrictions on the full range of motion.

Client Assessment, Reassessment, and Treatment Planning

Consultation

Although the most important consultation will occur at the beginning of the therapeutic relationship, a massage therapist still needs to include some consultation in every meeting with a client. To begin with, the therapist needs to find out how the self-care regimen is going. If there has been any change in the client's medical status, the therapist needs to be informed of this at the beginning of the session. Also, the therapist should solicit feedback about the last session. It is always a good idea to review the short-term and long-term goals of treatment and to ensure that the client is confident and optimistic about reaching these goals. Finally, every massage session should include an opportunity for the client to bring up any issues he or she feels are relevant to treatment.

Intake forms

Most massage therapists have their clients fill out what is called an intake form during the first appointment; the completed form contains the client's entire medical history. The form includes information about past problems, current health information, and a history of illness, injury, and medical procedures. Many massage therapists include an informed consent section as part of the intake form. If the client is on any medication, this should be indicated on the intake form. The intake form is also a good place to record the client's basic personal identification information, including their name, date of birth, address, and telephone number. It is a good idea to store intake forms in an accessible location so that they can be updated in the future.

SOAP form

Most massage therapists use what is called a SOAP form to record information about individual massage sessions. The name is an acronym for the four sections of the form: Subjective, Objective, Activity, and Plan. In the subjective section, the massage therapist lists the description given by the client. In the objective section, the massage therapist lists all of his or her important observations, including the results of the postural assessment, range of motion assessment, and gait assessment. In the activity section, the massage therapist describes the procedures that were performed during the session. In the plan section, the massage therapist indicates the future activities that should be performed in subsequent sessions.

Anterior postural assessment

A comprehensive postural assessment begins with an anterior postural assessment, in which the massage therapist looks at the front of the client's body. The assessment is performed by evaluating a series of physical landmarks. First, a massage therapist will note whether the ears are at the same level; then, he or she will check to see if the nose and chin lie on the midsagittal line. The massage therapist will then check to see if the clavicles are even and whether the sternum and belly button fall on the midsagittal line. The therapist then checks to see if the hands, which are dropped by the client's side, are at the same level, and whether the arches of the feet are roughly symmetrical. Any deviations should be noted on the postural assessment form.

Posterior postural assessment

After assessing a client's anterior posture, the massage therapist will need to assess the posterior and lateral postures. A posterior assessment begins in the same manner as the anterior assessment: checking to see if the client's ears are level. The therapist will then check to see if the client's shoulders form a line that is parallel to the ground and whether the spine appears to run along the midsagittal line. As with the anterior assessment, the next step of the posterior assessment is to determine whether the client's pelvis is level and whether his or her hands dangle to the same height. Finally, the therapist will assess the client's legs to determine whether the musculature is flexed in a symmetrical manner and whether the client's weight seems to be evenly distributed between his or her feet.

Lateral postural assessment

After completing the anterior and posterior postural assessments, the massage therapist will need to perform the lateral postural assessment. This begins by determining whether the client's head is properly positioned. The ears should be slightly behind the vertical reference line, which runs just in front of the lateral malleolus. The client's shoulders should be centered directly on the vertical reference line, and his or her hands should naturally face in the medial direction. Finally, the client's knees should be positioned so that the middle of the joint is on the vertical reference line. In general, the lateral postural assessment confirms problems with posture that were noted during the anterior and posterior assessments. The most common problem noted during a lateral postural assessment is that the head and neck are bent too far forward.

Gait assessment

Typically, a massage therapist will follow up the postural assessment with a brief gait assessment (walking assessment). The client will be directed to slowly walk in a straight line. The massage therapist will need to observe the client from the front, back, and side in order to collect the proper information. The client should be instructed to walk as naturally as possible. The therapist will be looking for even, symmetrical steps. The weight should be directed away from the arches of the feet. The therapist will also be looking to see if the client's head is positioned properly (above the spine) and if the shoulders are held back. The arms should swing away from the body at the exact same length and speed, and each knee should bend the same amount during a step.

Palpation assessment

During an introductory assessment of a new client, the massage therapist will need to use palpation to determine the client's problems and needs. Palpation is the use of touch to identify the structural characteristics of an individual's body. When a massage therapist performs a palpation assessment, he or she is primarily focusing on four elements: temperature, texture, movement, and rhythm. It's important to use light touch while performing a palpation assessment. Also, any palpation done on one side of the body should also be done on the other side. Palpation may be either superficial or, if necessary, quite deep. A deep palpation should not be performed unless it is necessary, as it may be painful for the client.

Basic range of motion assessment

The basic range of motion assessment is an essential part of the introductory massage session. There are two components of this assessment: active range of motion assessment and passive range of motion assessment. During the active range of motion assessment, the client will be flexing his or her joints without any assistance. The client should move slowly, and the only joint in motion should be the one being assessed. The client should proceed until he or she feels significant resistance, whether in the form of pain or tension. During a passive range of motion assessment, which is performed after the active range of motion assessment, the massage therapist will manipulate the joint without any assistance from the client. While manipulating the client's joints, the massage therapist should use gentle pressure and be responsive to any indications of pain or stress.

Temperature and texture of tissue

When performing a palpation assessment, the massage therapist will be sensitive to changes in temperature and tissue texture. The temperature of tissue is a good indicator of circulation. Warm tissue is receiving adequate blood flow, while tissue may be cold in areas affected by ischemia. As for texture, it is common for healthy muscles to move freely and feel firm but yielding. A tense muscle, on the other hand, will be knotty and resistant to movement. A healthy muscle will expand and yield in response to external pressure, while an unhealthy muscle will seem to melt away when force is applied. Moreover, an unhealthy muscle will be more likely to hurt when pressure is applied to it.

Movement and rhythm

A thorough palpation assessment will include tests to determine range of motion. It is typical for a massage therapist to palpate a joint as it is in motion. For example, the therapist might palpate the elbow as the arm is bending. If a muscle is resistant to movement or cannot relax enough to allow a normal range of motion, this is an indication of hypertonic muscle tissue. During the palpation assessment, the massage therapist must be aware of the client's breathing rhythm, heart rate, and craniosacral rhythm. It is better for the client's breathing to be slow and deep than shallow and fast. As a client relaxes, his or her breathing should slow down and deepen. It is also a good idea to check the heart rate at different points in the body, as restricted blood flow may be indicated by a slower pulse. The craniosacral flow is the motion of cerebrospinal fluid around the spinal cord and brain. It can be checked by palpating the occipital, parietal, and temporal bones.

Basic components of a treatment plan

After assessing the client and performing an initial treatment, the massage therapist and client will work together to develop a treatment plan. In order to be considered complete, a plan for future treatment needs to include the following information: proposed length of treatment (including frequency and duration of sessions), treatment techniques to be used, recommendations for self-care, and any supplemental care required by the patient. The treatment plan must be agreed upon by both the massage therapist and the client. Oftentimes, a massage therapist and client will develop a list of short-term and long-term goals, in part so that the client can recognize the gains that are being made through regular massage therapy.

<u>Length of treatment</u>
When developing a plan for future treatment, a massage therapist and his or her clients need to agree upon the appropriate duration and frequency of future sessions. In order to do this, it will be necessary to ascertain the amount of healing time the client will require between sessions. Clients who are under a great deal of stress or in bad health will require more healing time between sessions. If an individual is in good health, eats well, and has a relatively low stress lifestyle, he or she can be scheduled for more frequent and longer sessions. In the initial session, the massage therapist should be conscious of the point at which the client begins to experience pain. With this in mind, future sessions should be scheduled so that they will not run too long. Encouraging clients to maintain a healthy lifestyle outside of the massage environment will enable them to receive more treatment and better results from treatment.

Adjustments to a treatment plan

The initial plan for future treatment will probably be devised during the first or second massage therapy session, so it is natural for the plan to require adjustment as more information is acquired. Also, regular massage therapy will produce internal changes in the client, which may affect his or her requirements on the table. Over time, clients may develop affinities for particular techniques, which can be used more frequently during subsequent sessions. Finally, as clients begin to achieve their short-term and long-term goals, they may develop other reasons for wishing to continue massage therapy. It is a good idea to consult with a client regularly to ensure that the treatment plan is still appropriate and to make any necessary changes to improve individual results.

Overview of Massage and Bodywork Modalities/Culture/History

History of Massage Practices

China

Ancient Chinese documents contain a wealth of information about massage, which apparently began to be practiced around 3000 B.C.E. The Chinese primarily used a system of touch called *anmo*, in which the flesh was manipulated with a combination of pressure and friction. Over time, Chinese massage therapists incorporated a practice known as *tui-na*, which literally means pushing and pulling. Tui-na was often combined with acupuncture, tai chi, and qigong. These massage techniques were part of a comprehensive health program, which also included exercise, nutrition, and medicinal herbs. The practice of acupuncture developed out of Chinese massage.

India, Japan, and Egypt

The ancient Indian text known as the *Ayur Veda* describes a system of hand rubbing and massage hygiene that was designed to improve circulation. Massage was incorporated into the system of stretches and exercises that evolved into yoga. This text was written between 1000 and 3000 B.C.E. In Japan, massage was not practiced until 600 A.D., at which time the technique of finger pressure known as *shiatsu* was developed. In Egypt, there are records of massage treatments dating back as far as 4000 B.C.E. Apparently, the members of the royal family received massage treatments to improve their health.

Ancient Greece

In ancient Greece, there was no mind/body duality; people assumed that, in order to have good mental health, it was necessary to be physically fit. The ancient Greeks revered massage therapy as an important part of health maintenance, along with exercise, nutrition, hygiene, and relaxation practices. The Greek baths offered full body massage treatment from trained masseuses. Athletes, in particular, were advised to partake in frequent massage to improve their performance on the field. The comprehensive program of health which incorporated exercise, hygienic practices, and massage was known as gymnastics. Both men and women partook in these activities.

Renaissance

After the fall of the Roman Empire, in which the ancient Greek customs of massage were practiced, the practice of massage therapy lay dormant for centuries. During the Renaissance (beginning roughly in 1450 A.D.), however, scholars began to promote the health benefits of regular massage therapy in their writings. The anatomical drawings completed by da Vinci and Vesalius gave massage therapists new insights into the musculature and physiology of the human body. Furthermore, doctors began to see the benefits of physically manipulating body tissue, which included stimulating circulation and improving vitality.

Per Henrik Ling

The Swedish physiologist Per Henrik Ling (1776-1839) is credited with ushering in the modern era of massage therapy. He developed the system of rhythmic symmetrical movements known as Swedish gymnastics, which incorporated muscular strength training, muscular endurance training, and flexibility exercises. Ling advocated repetitive movements incorporating both sides of the body, and gradually introduced a system of massage-like manipulations which came to be known as Swedish massage. Although these techniques bear little resemblance to the massage therapy practiced today, they are credited with reviving interest in massage therapy.

19th-century America

In the United States during the 19th century, a sudden increased interest in health led to a revival of massage techniques. American doctors and fitness instructors introduced the Swedish massage techniques and added their own. The American physician John Harvey Kellogg (1852-1943) developed an extensive system of massage that paid attention to the various effects that massage had on the mechanics, reflexes, and metabolism of the body. His published work brought considerable attention to the health benefits of massage. Around the same time, the terminology of massage was being developed by a Dutch physician named Johann Mezger. Mezger is responsible for developing the important massage terms effleurage and pétrissage.

20th century

The 20th century has seen rapid developments in massage therapy, as well as a stunning growth in the number of distinct fields of practice. Many of the New Age movements of the 1960s endorsed massage as a means of unlocking human potential. More generally, though, doctors and exercise physiologists have continued to accumulate a body of research data describing the many positive effects of massage. Over the past 50 years, a number of professional organizations (including the American Massage Therapy Association) have been formed to advance the profession of massage therapy.

Swedish massage

Swedish massage is based on the physiological insights of Per Henrik Ling. Presently, it is the most common form of massage practiced in the United States. It involves the use of the hands, elbows, and lower arms. During a Swedish massage, the flesh of the client is kneaded and vigorously manipulated in order to increase circulation, promote relaxation, and diminish stress. Swedish massage includes several different kinds of strokes: effleurage (long, superficial strokes); pétrissage (kneading); tapotement (gentle beating); and rubbing. Research consistently shows that Swedish massage increases the flow of blood and lymphatic fluid throughout the body.

Types of Massages

Neuromuscular massage

Neuromuscular massage emphasizes pressure applied to the so-called "trigger points" on the body. Trigger points are areas where the nervous system can be stimulated through light touch. These points correspond to other areas of the body that can be healed through attention to the trigger points. Neuromuscular massage typically entails applying moderate pressure to the trigger points for prolonged periods of time. The goals of neuromuscular therapy are to reduce pain, correct problems with posture, and enhance range of motion. The term "neuromuscular" reflects the attention this technique gives to the interrelationship between the nervous and muscular systems.

Circulatory massage

Although most massage ends up improving the body's circulation, there are some modalities which have this as their central aim. The goal of circulatory massage is to improve the circulation of blood, lymphatic fluid, and waste products. Circulatory massage incorporates a variety of mechanical techniques that stimulate the flow of blood by improving the performance of arteries and veins. Also, there are a number of lymph drainage techniques that initiate the movement of lymph from the body tissues to the heart. A trained massage therapist will also be able to stimulate the evacuation of waste by applying specific types of pressure to the lower intestine.

Energy massage

Two of the most common forms of energy massage are Reiki and polarity therapy. Reiki aims to support the flow of energy throughout the body. The practice of Reiki is relatively easy to learn; very little formal training is required. Polarity therapy, meanwhile, seeks to improve health by making adjustments to the energy field that surrounds every human being. According to practitioners of polarity therapy, the natural circulation of electrical energy around the human body can be obstructed by imperfect body processes. These obstructions may be caused by poor posture, mood disorders, or muscular tension. The practitioner of polarity therapy tries to restore the electrical field around the subject so that he or she can regain normal energy flow.

Movement massage

Movement massage modalities oblige the client to take a more active role in his or her therapy. Some of the most common varieties of movement massage are Feldenkrais, Trager, and Alexander. Feldenkrais emphasizes relearning common movement patterns in such a way that they diminish the stresses placed on certain parts of the body. The Alexander technique is specifically aimed at improving posture and balance by forcing the client to become conscious of habitual movements. This method is especially popular among actors and dancers because of the control it gives the client over his or her body. The Trager system encourages clients to move their bodies as a therapist applies light pressure to certain key areas; this technique is good for relieving muscular tension.

Structural and postural integration massage

Structural and postural integration modalities emphasize the importance of developing and maintaining proper body alignment when standing and performing normal movements. Two of the most common modalities in this category are Rolfing and Hellerwork. Rolfing focuses on improving posture through a systematic reshaping of the body's myofascial structure. A certified "Rolfer" administers light pressure all over the body with his or her fingers, elbows, and knuckles. The goal is to relax the muscles until they reach their natural state of alignment. Hellerwork, meanwhile, focuses on releasing built-up tension in the connective tissues. According to this discipline, the body becomes used to destructive misalignment and requires massage to regain its natural structure.

Oriental massage

Oriental massage modalities emphasize the flow of energy through the body. According to their theories, the unrestricted flow of energy supports good health. Some of the most common modalities in this category are Acupressure and Shiatsu massage. Acupressure, as the name indicates, is a combination of acupuncture and massage. It involves the application of light pressure to the points of the body which, in acupuncture, are pierced with needles. Shiatsu is a similar therapy that involves treating the entire body. Shiatsu theory asserts that by restoring the overall health of the body, particular areas of stress and tension can be alleviated. Shiatsu involves the application of light pressure to the acupuncture sites in the hope that it will restore effective energy flow through the body.

Reflexology

Reflexology is a study that involves stimulating certain parts of the body to produce a reaction in other parts of the body. It is based on the principal that every organ within the body has a corresponding point on either the hands or feet. By applying pressure to the ball of the foot, for example, the practitioner can produce a favorable reaction within the lungs and heart. In addition to the organs, reflexology can also affect glands and muscles. Through the application of pressure to the areas corresponding to these glands, tension can be relieved, and there may be an overall increase in body function. As an example, the heel of the foot is believed to correspond to the lower back. Pressure on the big toe can lead to relief from headaches. It is important to understand that some skeptics do not believe that this type of massage is beneficial. In any case, practitioners should not project the opinion that reflexology is a medical cure-all.

Chair massage

Chair massage originated in Japan and is believed to be several centuries old. It is a form of massage that has become increasingly popular. It can be found in shopping malls, airports, workplaces, convention centers, and other areas where large numbers of people congregate. Chair massage allows the client to be fully clothed while sitting in a chair in a semi-reclined, prone position. Chair massage is an effective way to introduce massage to a person who may exhibit adverse reactions to touch and is also suitable for those who may consider traditional Swedish massage too invasive.

<u>Advantages of chair massage</u>
Chair massage is often an introduction to massage therapy for individuals who, for one reason or another, are apprehensive about the process. Chair massage is sometimes used as a way to introduce positive reactions to touch. It may be suitable for those who have been victims of sexual, physical, or emotional abuse. The chair massage technique enables the practitioner to complete a

session in less than 30 minutes, thus making it readily accessible to those on a tight schedule. Finally, chair massage is more cost-effective than standard massage sessions, allowing it to be used by people who are less inclined or able to spend money on weekly massages.

Procedure for performing chair massage
Due to the high volume of massages being performed by chair massage practitioners, the initial consultation will likely be shorter than in a standard therapeutic setting. However, the practitioner should still screen for any contraindications to the massage prior to commencement. As the client is fully clothed and seated in a prone position, certain techniques, including effleurage and gliding, are not possible. Due to the nature of chair massage, friction, percussion, and deep touches are the only appropriate techniques. With the client seated in the prone position, the head, neck, shoulders, back, and hips may be the only areas the practitioner can access.

Special considerations and hygienic practices
Some chair massages require the therapist to take special considerations into account in order to provide adequate therapeutic benefits to the client. In some cases, the client is seated in a supine position to enable the therapist to gain access to the lower legs and feet to perform massage in those areas. After each client leaves, the practitioner must ensure the chair meets standards of cleanliness before the next client is seated. Wiping down areas that come into contact with the client's skin with an anti-bacterial cleanser is important to control transmission of bacteria or germs. As an alternative, disposable coverings for the face cushion can be used.

Lymph massage

Lymph massage is closely related to Swedish massage. It is designed to assist with the movement of the lymphatic fluids within the body. When lymph nodes are filled with fluid, a condition known as lymphedema, physicians sometimes recommend lymph drainage massage as a means of alleviating the symptoms. Specific methods designed to assist with the flow of lymph fluids can cause an increase in metabolism, drain stagnant fluids and toxins, and stimulate the immune system. The rhythmic movements used in lymph massage also stimulate the parasympathetic nervous system which, in turn, helps to relieve stress, depression, and insomnia. Lymph massage can also help rebalance the chemistry within the body, assist in tissue regeneration, normalize organs, and boost the immune system. When done correctly, the procedure entails gentle, slow movements that are performed over the lymph nodes in a circular pattern. Light pressure is then applied in the direction of lymph flow to direct the movement of lymph.

Deep tissue massage

Deep tissue massage targets the tissues of the body that are below the superficial musculature. Some of the most common forms of deep tissue massage include cross-fiber friction, connective tissue massage, craniosacral massage, and myofascial massage. A deep tissue massage generally includes long strokes of moderate intensity and prolonged periods of pressure to certain points on the body. In order to apply direct contact to the deep muscles of the body, a certain degree of relaxation must be achieved. Therefore, it may take a while before attention can be directed to the deep muscles. Deep tissue massage can be painful, so the client should be monitored closely during each session.

Deep tissue massage refers to the massage style that focuses on the deeper muscles and fascia tissues. Various techniques are used in this form of massage to alleviate any tension in the muscular fibers. Massage of this nature can also contribute to psychological and physiological changes in the body. These therapeutic techniques may require long warm-up periods before the deep tissues of the client can be accessed. The intent behind this type of massage is to loosen the bonds between the layers of connective tissue. Some of the popular deep massage techniques are Rolfing, Trager, Hellerwork, and Feldenkrais.

Rolfing

One type of deep tissue massage, known as Rolfing, is named after Dr. Ida Rolf, the woman who developed the technique. She devised this technique to alleviate tension and structural problems caused by years of poor posture and alignment. Rolfing utilizes a heavy-handed technique to realign the body. Performed over a series of many treatments, the massage therapist uses his or her hands, fists, or even knuckles to align the body's movements and create a sense of balance within. A full treatment of Rolfing involves a series of 10 treatments, although fewer treatments can also lead to improvement.

Trigger point therapy

Trigger points in the body refer to skeletal muscle areas that are hyperirritable. The presence of palpable nodules in the bands of muscle fibers sometimes causes pain responses that can refer to other parts of the body. Trigger points are classified according to their location in the body and whether or not pain is felt upon palpitation. A common trigger point site is an acupuncture site, though some trigger points are located elsewhere on the body. Activation of a trigger point can be caused by an increase in stress levels, overuse of a particular muscle, and even an arthritic condition. A brief listing of common trigger points is given below:
- Active myofascial trigger point
- Latent myofascial trigger point
- Central trigger point
- Attachment trigger point
- Primary (or key) trigger point
- Satellite trigger point
- Associate trigger point

Acupressure

Similar in theory to acupuncture, acupressure is a Chinese technique in which pressure is applied from the hand, elbow, or fingers to acupuncture points across the body. The purpose of acupressure is to relieve the body by balancing the physical and psychological aspects. Through this method, a person can experience an increase in circulatory function and an enhanced ability to manage pain. Acupressure is usually part of an overall health regimen that also incorporates a healthy diet, exercise, and meditation. The overall goal is to develop a holistic lifestyle. Areas of the body where pressure points may be found are along the crown of the head, the temple, the forehead, and the upper jaw. Other areas can include the sides and front of the neck, upper arms, elbow joint, and the outside of the thighs and lower legs. Areas that commonly experience feelings of relief through acupressure include the toes, metatarsals, ankles, heels, and Achilles tendon.

Hydrotherapy, heat therapy, and cold treatments

Hydrotherapy is the practice of using water in its liquid, gas, or solid forms as part of a massage therapy treatment plan. Heat therapy can involve the application of dry heat, moist heat, or diathermy. Dry heat involves the use of heating pads, infrared radiation, or a sauna. Moist heat can come from an immersion bath, spray, heat packs, or a steam bath. Diathermy can entail the transmission of shortwave or microwave electromagnetic fields onto the tissue. The purpose of heat therapy is to cause vessels to dilate and increase circulation. Care must be taken to closely monitor the client's body temperature. Cold therapy is also known as cryotherapy. This technique is performed to help reduce the edema, swelling, and pain accompanying an injury. Cold treatments should be applied for short periods of time due to the possibility of tissue injury from the cold. Examples of cold treatments are immersion baths, ice packs, ice massage, mechanical compressors, and vasocoolant sprays.

When used as a method of therapy, water can be used in any of its three forms: solid, liquid, or gaseous vapor. When cold water is used for hydrotherapy, it has the immediate effect of cooling the skin and drawing blood away from the surface of the body. The nerves experience a reduction in their sensitivity levels and the activity of the body's cells in that particular area begins to slow down. After these initial reactions take place, a secondary reaction occurs, which causes the skin to become warmer and more relaxed. The blood cells on the surface of the skin begin to expand again and nerve impulses increase. The activity level of nearby cells increases. When heat therapy is conducted, reactions that occur cause the blood cells from the interior of the body to move towards the surface of the skin, which produces a reddish area on the skin. These blood vessels dilate and cause an increase in circulation. The body's temperature rises, and sweating may occur. All of these changes serve to relax the blood vessels, nerves, and muscles.

Aromatherapy

Aromatherapy is the use of essential oils from natural herbs, flowers, and spices to enhance the massage experience through the sense of smell. These aromas can bring about a specific reaction, and are commonly chosen to augment the massage session. Some of the most popular essential oils are chamomile, eucalyptus, jasmine, lavender, and lemongrass. The effects these oils produce can be calming, stimulating, refreshing, or relaxing. It is not a good idea to use these essential oils at their full strength. Instead, they should be combined with another medium, such as carrier oil. This oil serves as a lubricant and helps to blend the oil so it is not overly concentrated, which can cause irritation. Aromatherapy can also involve the use of scented candles or lotion. Prior to the massage, the therapist should consult the intake form or ask the client verbally about any allergies or sensitivities to oils or aromas that may be used during the massage.

Body wraps

Body wraps are used for different purposes, including relaxation, detoxification, and cleansing and softening the skin. Various substances can be used in the wraps, including seaweed, volcanic clay, and mud. Heat is a common element of wraps, whether it comes from an outside source or is obtained from the body. Contraindicators for wraps include high blood pressure, heart disease, and pregnancy. Body wraps are beneficial in that they provide comfort, security, and warmth, and also allow the nutrients to be absorbed in a closed environment instead of being dispersed through the air.

Technique for performing a body wrap
When performing a body wrap, the practitioner must be aware of factors that may prevent the client from being fully wrapped. The practitioner must also take precautions when determining the temperature level of the wrap. The table is laid out with a blanket, a thermal blanket, a towel, and finally, a plastic wrap. The client lies down on this plastic and an exfoliation is performed on the client's skin prior to the application of the seaweed or mud. As the seaweed or mud is brushed over

the body, the practitioner wraps that portion of the body to prevent heat from escaping. Upon completion, the client is completely engulfed in wraps and is allowed to relax for some time before being assisted through the clean-up process by the therapist.

Exfoliation procedure

An exfoliation procedure can be performed in a massage therapy room. In this instance, the body is moistened with a sponge rather than in a shower or bath. After the body has been moistened, the practitioner puts salts or exfoliates into his hands and applies them in a circular fashion over the body. Only one surface is exfoliated at a time. A wet towel is used to wipe off the salts, and then a wet loofah is used to apply soap to the body. After the body has been cleansed, another hot, wet cloth is used to remove all residue of soap. The body is then dried off with another towel, and the practitioner then applies moisturizer all over the body. Exfoliation using salts from the Dead Sea is similar in nature, except the salts are mixed with water to form a paste prior to applying them to the body.

Athletic or sports massage

Athletic massage is used to help treat athletic injuries, which increases the level of strength training, conditioning, and activity. The sports massage therapist must be knowledgeable about anatomy, physiology, kinesiology, and biomechanics in order to help the athlete return to the level of conditioning required for his sport. Biomechanics refers to the movement of the body. Soft tissue injuries commonly account for a large portion of the injuries seen by the sports massage therapist. Sports massage therapists must have knowledge of the various muscle groups and how they are used within the sport. It is also important for him to understand the functions of the circulatory system and the nervous system, as they also interact with the muscles.

Beneficial effects
The main effects of an athletic massage are:
- Oxygen is more readily available, which allows for repair of the injured body part.
- Waste materials are flushed out by increased circulation, causing increased energy levels.
- The muscles, ligaments, and tendons are stretched, allowing for greater flexibility.
- The occurrence of muscle spasms is reduced.
- Adhesions are broken down within the muscle, resulting in less scar tissue formation after an injury.
- Collagen fibers come into alignment, leading to a stronger healed area.
- The likelihood of future injuries is reduced.
- Acids are released from the body, which causes the muscles to "bounce" back after an intense workout.
- The career of an athlete can potentially be extended because they may sustain fewer injuries.

When performing a warm-up massage on an athlete, it is important to note any potential problems that could lead to a more serious, debilitating injury. If an injury does occur, massage can help to alleviate the common problems associated with the injury. Massage is an effective means of reducing edema and swelling of the affected joint or area. The time that the body needs to recover from the injury is minimized. The scar tissue that is formed at the site of the injury is more flexible, which means the tissue is less stiff. The athlete can develop an increased range of motion in the affected limb as a result of continued massage. The athlete stands a greater chance of returning to full form more quickly than if massage was not included as part of the rehabilitation program.

Components of athletic massage

An athletic massage is broken down into four parts: pre-event massage, post-event massage, restorative or training massage, and rehabilitation massage. Pre-event massage is used before a competition to prepare and invigorate the athlete for the rigors of a competition. It is usually given between 15 minutes to 4 hours before a competition to increase flexibility and circulation. A post-event massage helps to cool the body down and restore the tissues to their normal state. The kneading, compression, and light stretching also helps to relax the athlete. A restorative massage is used during training and includes deep cross-fiber friction and joint stretches. Rehabilitation massage is used to help heal and repair muscle tissue after an injury. This type of massage shortens the recuperative time and also prevents any scar tissue from forming. It helps build a stronger muscle or joint, and also allows the athlete to return to training with less likelihood of re-injury.

Ethics, Boundaries, Laws, Regulations

Accountability

A massage therapist must demonstrate accountability, the ability to take on the responsibilities of a professional. Being accountable means taking responsibility when massage therapy produces an adverse reaction, as well as taking credit for the positive consequences of therapy. In order to be truly accountable, one needs to fully understand the scope of the practice of massage therapy, as well as the code of ethics that must be followed by professionals. Only by understanding the rules of professional practice and the limitations on a massage therapist can one truly take responsibility and be accountable.

Ethical issues

Sooner or later, you will be required to resolve an ethical issue in your professional practice. This issue may or may not have arisen because of your own conduct. Nevertheless, it is your responsibility as an ethical professional to do everything within your power to resolve the issue. First, you should gather as much information as you need to make an informed decision. You should then determine who will be affected by your decision. If necessary, you should contact relevant law enforcement authorities. You may also find it helpful to consult the code of ethics for your jurisdiction. Finally, you should make what you consider to be the ethical decision, and then explain your decision and its consequences to all relevant parties.

Personal boundaries

Boundaries are defined as the personal comfort zones that each person maintains for his own security. Boundaries are intangible and unseen. The acceptable distance from one person's body to another individual varies and is dependent on each individual's personal preferences. Boundaries can be divided into four types: physical, emotional, intellectual, and sexual. They serve as a personal protective device and, during the course of the massage, the practitioner should be aware of any subtle nuances that would let him know that the client may be on the verge of discomfort. It is important that the practitioner be aware of the client's boundaries, and it is vital that they exhibit the utmost respect, concern, and professionalism at all times.

Professional boundaries

There are eight issues related to professional boundaries. They include:
- Location of services received – This refers to the location at which massage services are received. Boundaries are less likely to be crossed when the client's safety, comfort, and security are taken into consideration.
- Interpersonal space – This refers to the distance between the practitioner and the client. For sensitive individuals, it is one of the boundaries crossed most frequently.
- Appearance – The impression the massage therapist practitioner makes on their clients is influenced by their appearance. Good hygiene and modest clothing promote a sense of professionalism.
- Self-disclosure – Any personal information provided by the client to the practitioner should be directly related to the treatment and therapy at hand.

- Language- The choice of words, tone, phrasing, and intonation help to create a safe, secure, peaceful environment.
- Touch – Touch during a massage is necessary. However, skin-to-skin contact should only occur at the parts of the body that are being massaged. The genital area is to be avoided, and draping should be provided for all areas not being massaged.
- Time – Adherence to set appointment times shows respect for the client's time and other personal activities. Also, open communication regarding policies for missed appointments, no shows, and lateness helps to define the boundaries between the client and the practitioner.
- Money – Defining the fee schedule for services rendered in advance of the therapeutic sessions helps to define boundaries. Charging various fees based on a person's skin color, gender, relationship status, etc. does not reflect the type of professionalism all healthcare professionals should be trying to achieve.

Code of ethics

A code of ethics defines the roles and responsibilities assigned to the members of a given profession. Many of the professional organizations for massage therapists have issued codes of ethics. These codes are all somewhat different but contain a few common elements. Massage therapists are required to strive to provide the best service to their clients but to never administer treatment for which they have not been trained. Massage therapists are forbidden from practicing any form of discrimination when they deal with clients. They are required to obey all of the laws in their jurisdiction and to accept responsibility for their actions. They are required to act professionally at all times and to avoid conflicts of interest and unprofessional relationships with clients.

Therapeutic relationship

The relationship between a massage therapist and his or her clients is often described as a therapeutic relationship: one in which one person is responsible for improving the health and quality of life of another person in exchange for money. There is a subtle dynamic at work in this relationship, however, and therapists need to be aware of this. For one thing, it is essential to note that the client is in a significantly weaker position in the relationship. He or she is unlikely to know much about the treatment, will be placed in various compromising positions throughout the therapy, and will have to rely on the professionalism and efficacy of the therapist. The therapist should be conscious of the fact that the client has placed him or herself in a vulnerable position voluntarily and should make sure that the client's trust has been well placed. The therapist is responsible for upholding the highest professional standards and not taking advantage of the power he or she holds over the client.

Dual relationships

Occasionally, you may be required to manage a dual relationship in your professional practice. In other words, you may be required to provide professional services for a person with whom you already have a personal relationship. This is not necessarily an ethical quandary, so long as both parties are aware of the restrictions on the relationship during professional service. So long as you perform your duties as a professional according to the standards set by your employer and the relevant professional associations, it should not matter whether you are providing therapy to a friend or relative. However, you should be sure to treat your friends and family as you would any other valued client. You should also be sure that they, in turn, treat you with the respect you are owed as a professional.

Sexuality issues

Massage is a sensual activity, and so a massage therapist needs to be careful to maintain appropriate sexual boundaries during his or her professional work. At no time should a massage therapist come into direct contact with the genitalia of their clients. It is not uncommon for a client to become sexually aroused during the course of a massage. This is only natural, as massage tends to stimulate the parasympathetic nervous system and direct more blood flow to the genitals. One way to deal with this problem is to deliver more rapid, drumming strokes to the body, which tends to stifle arousal. Another strategy is to simply explain to the client the physiological reasons for his or her arousal and leave it at that. It is not considered sexual harassment to simply describe to a client the natural changes that occur during massage, so long as no effort is made to violate the boundary between client and therapist.

Educational requirements for certification

There are no mandated national educational requirements for certification or licensure as a massage therapist. However, there are certain elements required for certification that are common among all jurisdictions. For instance, almost all states require applicants to have a high school diploma or GED. Most licensing organizations require at least 500 hours of instruction in massage therapy, with emphasis on anatomy, physiology, pathology, modalities of bodywork and massage, contraindications for massage, massage safety, and professional practice. Usually, individuals are required to pass a standardized test in order to receive their license. There are a few different standardized tests used throughout the United States for this purpose.

Revocation or suspension of license

If you violate the code of ethics or regulations set by the governing body, you may have your massage therapist's license revoked or suspended. For instance, if you are convicted of a felony while practicing as a massage therapist, your license may be suspended. The following events can also be cause for the revocation or suspension of a license: prostitution, willful negligence, substance abuse, deceptive advertising, and sexual misconduct in the line of duty. Furthermore, if the organization that issued your license determines that you used deception in order to obtain a license, it may be revoked.

Scope of practice

A scope of practice is the list of activities a given professional has the right to perform under on his or her license. The precise description of a massage therapist's scope of practice is different in every state. It is important for a therapist to understand his or her scope of practice so that he or she does not overstep professional boundaries. The scope of practice for wellness massage is smaller than that for therapeutic massage. This is because the goals of wellness massage are more general and less ambitious. In order to practice wellness massage, a massage therapist must have general training in the anatomy, physiology, pathology, and modalities of wellness massage. He or she is then authorized to use these modalities to promote circulation and reduce stress.

Informed consent forms

Since the massage therapist understands his or her professional business much better than his or her clients, it is the responsibility of the therapist to describe in detail any proposed treatment before initiation. This is done by means of an informed consent form, in which the proposed treatment is described in full, including any potential risks of the treatment. The presentation of an informed consent document gives the client a chance to ask questions. An informed consent form may also include a list of actions which would result in the immediate termination of treatment; it is a good idea for the therapist to publish such a list in the event that a dispute with the client arises.

Professional communication skills

One of the most important but least talked about aspects of ethical professional practice as a massage therapist is effective communication. In order to serve a client, the therapist needs to be able to describe his or her work and understand the concerns, complaints, and questions of the client. The therapist needs to establish a relationship with the client in which the client feels comfortable making requests and offering constructive criticism. Too often, massage therapists cultivate their reputations as experts to such a degree that a client does not feel comfortable asking for what he or she wants. In order to effectively serve his or her clients, a therapist needs to be able to listen without judgment. Furthermore, the client's goals should always be the primary consideration when the therapist is making decisions.

Initial consultations

The initial consultation is perhaps the most important session in any therapeutic story because it establishes the relationship between the therapist and the client. In order to get the most out of this and any subsequent consultations, a therapist needs to be able to ask pertinent and effective questions. It is important for the therapist to establish an environment in which the client feels comfortable discussing his or her health. The therapist should remember that many clients will not have a vocabulary for what they are trying to express, and so the therapist should help draw their feelings out without dominating the conversation or distorting the client's point of view. A therapist should ask questions which give the client a chance to ruminate on his or her health history and should seek to clarify any uncertain points by asking specific, objective questions.

Nonverbal communication

Because massage therapy is a profession concerned with touch, it is not surprising that some of the most important communication between massage therapists and clients is nonverbal. Nonverbal communication is not limited to touch, however. In order to establish a positive working relationship with a client, a massage therapist needs to communicate warmth and accessibility with his or her body language. A smile and a relaxed posture can be contagious and can help a client derive extra benefits from a massage session. Also, a therapist needs to consider the body language of a client and should tread lightly when a client seems peevish or defensive. Additionally, a client's body language will sometimes give the therapist information about his or her condition that the client cannot express through words.

Confidentiality

A massage therapist is required to respect the privacy of his or her clients by maintaining strict confidentiality standards. This means keeping client records in a secure location, and not sharing them with other practitioners without the permission of the client. In order to provide health information to another professional, even the client's doctor, you must receive permission from the client. Confidentiality can only be violated when it is obvious that there is an immediate danger to the client or some other person. In some rare cases, a client may not want to be recognized outside of the therapy environment. If you are in public and notice that a client seems to be avoiding you, do not make special efforts to attract the attention of the client.

Guidelines for Professional Practice

Safety Practices

Appropriate hygiene regimen

In order to prevent infection and the spread of disease, a massage therapist needs to engage in a comprehensive hygiene regimen. The most important part of this regimen is handwashing after every client encounter. During handwashing, an antibacterial soap should be used. All jewelry should be removed from the hands. Alcohol-based hand sanitizers are an acceptable alternative. A therapist should also put on latex gloves whenever he or she is required to clean up the bodily fluids of a client. A therapist should clean his or her equipment regularly with antiseptics, and should occasionally use a stronger disinfectant, making sure to rinse the equipment thoroughly with warm water afterwards.

Contamination

Massage therapy can be a breeding ground for infection if the massage therapist is not careful. To maintain their clientele, a therapist must have a facility that is clean and sterile and must protect against the spread of disease to safeguard the well-being of their clients. Following strict laws regulating sanitation procedures, the massage therapist must utilize disinfectants, antiseptics, and other cleaning agents to maintain a healthy environment. Illness- and disease-causing pathogens are transmitted from one infected person to another directly or indirectly. They can enter the body through inhalation, ingestion, broken skin, contact with mucous membranes, or sexual contact.

Transmittal of pathogens

Pathogens can be transmitted through beverages or food. Types of pathogens the massage therapist should be concerned about are bacteria, fungus, and viruses. Bacteria are most commonly found on dirty surfaces and in unclean water and can cause illnesses such as pneumonia, typhoid fever, TB, diphtheria, and syphilis, just to name a few. Viruses can invade living hosts and transmit diseases such as colds, mumps, measles, and pneumonia. Warm, moist environments create an ideal environment for fungi and mold to reproduce. Fungal infections are responsible for ringworm, athlete's foot, and Candida.

Universal precautions

The following steps are considered necessary precautions to stop the spread of infection:
- Washing hands with soap and water before and after contact with each client
- Using disposable paper towels rather than cloth
- Washing skin and hands thoroughly if any contact is made with contaminated fluids
- Wearing gloves when performing certain tasks and washing hands after removing the gloves
- Washing any linens contaminated with blood or bodily fluids in hot water with bleach and drying them in a hot dryer

- Handling contaminated linens as little as possible and separating them from other linens
- Cleaning surfaces such as walls and ceilings with disinfectant if they come in contact with spills requiring sanitation

Maintenance of safe facilities

When we think of safety in the context of massage therapy, we usually think of the physical manipulations, which have the potential to stress and strain the body of the client or the therapist. However, it is equally important for the facilities at the massage therapist's office to be safe. By facilities, we mean all of the buildings, furnishings, and equipment used by the massage therapist and his or her customers. In order to maintain a high level of safety, a massage therapist needs to keep the buildings clean, uncluttered, well-lit, and sanitized. All equipment should be checked frequently to make sure it is sturdy and safe for use. Every massage office should have an accessible first-aid kit and the phone numbers for emergency services posted next to the telephone.

Maintaining client safety

The best way to maintain client safety is to have clean and safe facilities and to communicate any potential hazards to the client. For instance, clients should be alerted whenever the therapist is about to position his or her body in a potentially stressful manner. Disabled or elderly clients should be assisted into position and should also be helped on and off the massage table. Clients who are ill, injured, or have severe allergies should have these conditions thoroughly examined before undergoing massage therapy. In addition, a massage therapist needs to keep a fully-stocked first-aid kit on hand at all times in case the client should suffer some injury. In order to minimize the risk of infection, the massage therapist should wash his or her hands after every client.

Maintaining therapist safety

Although a massage therapist primarily focuses on improving the quality of life of his or her clients, the therapist also needs to protect him or herself from injury or illness. To this end, the therapist should wash his or her hands after every encounter with a client. The therapist should not perform any therapies that are outside his or her scope of expertise and should be aware of any counterindications for massage practice. In order to reduce the risk of infection in the massage environment, the therapist should clean and sterilize equipment with a disinfectant regularly. The therapist should also ensure that his or her work environment has adequate ventilation.

Physical health of massage therapist

A person considering massage therapy should understand that this profession requires a great deal of physical strength. To assist others through massage, the therapist places considerable stress on his own body, which can be injured if proper procedures are not followed when performing the massage on a client. Proper stances, exercises for the hands, and good body mechanics will help eliminate some of the stress on the practitioner. It is important to develop good posture, coordination, balance, and stamina to provide the best possible massages for the client with minimal damage to oneself. As the hands are the most important of the practitioner's tools, flexibility is key to controlling the speed of the massage and pressure sensitivity, along with the ability to conform to the contours of the client's body. Along with proper physical conditioning, the therapist should also concentrate on his emotional state during the massage and not let outside influences mar the session.

Body mechanics

In order to avoid injury and unnecessary strain on the body, a massage therapist needs to learn proper body mechanics. One of the main principles of body mechanics, as it applies to massage therapy, is leverage, the technique of producing the greatest amount of pressure on the client with the least amount of work. Basically, leverage is achieved in massage therapy by locking the arms at the elbows and leaning on the client so that the weight of the therapist is doing most of the work. Also, massage therapists should try to stand as close to their clients as possible, as proximity makes the work of creating pressure easier. In order to deliver effective force with the use of leverage, it is important for the massage table to be set low enough that the therapist can lean into the patient without his or her arm being at too much of an angle with his or her torso.

Symmetric and asymmetric stance

In order to avoid being injured as a result of the repetitive stresses associated with practicing massage therapy, one needs to learn the appropriate uses of the symmetric and asymmetric stances. In the symmetric stance, the feet are shoulder-width apart, with the knees flexed to the same degree and the toes pointed forward. This stance is appropriate when the client is directly in front of the therapist, as the weight is evenly distributed between the legs. In the asymmetric stance, on the other hand, one foot is in front of the other, with the front foot pointed forward and the back foot pointed slightly to the outside. In this pose, the majority of the weight is on the back foot. This stance is appropriate when the therapist is trying to get extra leverage to apply more pressure to the client's body. A massage therapist needs to be able to work comfortably with either the right or left foot forward in the asymmetric stance.

Poor body mechanics

Although massage therapy is primarily a gentle discipline, the repetitive movements and application of pressure can result in injury for therapists with poor body mechanics. In particular, the hands, wrists, and elbows are subject to a great deal of strain during massage. In order to avoid repetitive stress injuries, a therapist should keep the table at the appropriate height (such that the arms are almost fully extended when laid on the client) and avoid applying pressure with too great of an angle from the body. The therapist's back should be kept straight as much as possible, and his or her shoulders should remain back rather than hunched forward. Therapists should also slightly flex their knees and wear shoes that distribute their weight evenly throughout the foot.

Self-employed

One of the first decisions that must be made after being certified as a massage therapist is whether to go into business for oneself or work as an employee at a spa, doctor's office, or medical facility. There are pros and cons to each situation. Working as a self-employed massage therapist forces the practitioner to be responsible for paying his own employment taxes, paying for needed supplies (such as office equipment and the massage table), and assuming any rental costs for the facility. Disadvantages include the lack of a formal support team, being responsible for managing the paperwork for the business side as a self-employed entity, and the lack of a steady paycheck due to the time needed to build the business. Working in an established environment allows the therapist to have a built-in clientele, without incurring the overhead costs of doing business. Additionally, the therapist has the support of fellow employees to help with increased client loads. The company would also provide benefits such as vacation, sick leave, and health insurance, and would be responsible for paying any state and federal employer taxes.

Types of businesses

A massage therapist has the option of registering their business as a sole proprietor, partnership, limited liability corporation, or corporation. There are advantages and disadvantages to each of these arrangements. A sole proprietorship is a business in which the owner assumes all responsibility for the business, whether from a financial or obligatory standpoint. The individual is also legally responsible for all failures of the business and may be held accountable if any lawsuits are brought against the company. The courts will see the individual and the business as one entity. Therefore, the person is held legally responsible for any business debt. An advantage of a sole proprietorship is that the owner is not accountable to a board or group of shareholders.

Under a partnership, two or more individuals share in the successes and failures of the business; all partners share equally in the risk. It is similar to a sole proprietorship in that the group of owners can be held personally responsible for all activities of the business. A limited liability corporation (LLC) is a combination of a partnership and a corporation. A limited liability corporation has some of the same benefits as a corporation, but there is less paperwork involved. Additionally, an LLC offers more protection of one's personal assets in the event of a lawsuit. Finally, a corporation assigns management of the business to a board of directors who share in the policy development and decision-making processes. Stockholders are financially tied to the success of the company, as they share in any profits that are made.

Start-up expenses

As with any business, money is needed to buy the necessary office equipment and to help cover the costs of leasing space. Start-up expenses for a massage therapy practice can include the following:
- Work location – While leasing office space is more expensive than working from one's home, safety concerns may drive many therapists to find space to share with other therapists.
- Utilities – This refers to the costs associated with electricity, water, gas, phone lines, etc. that will be required in the work space.
- Massage therapy tables and other equipment – This can include portable as well as stationary massage tables and chairs, bolsters, towels and linens, and massage oils and lotions. It can also include any hydrotherapy tubs and other equipment used to perform percussive and vibratory movements on the client.

- Furniture – Desk and chairs are needed for the waiting area, office, and conference room. The massage therapist also requires a personal work desk.
- Office supplies – Required supplies could include a computer, fax machine, file cabinets, writing utensils, appointment books, etc.
- Advertising and printing expenses – These are the costs of marketing your massage therapy business, whether through print, TV, or radio advertisements.
- Insurance and licensing costs – These help the practitioner limit liabilities and ensure they are able to remain in business.

Licenses and permits

In order to successfully operate a business, several licenses must be obtained. These include:
- Fictitious name statement (DBA) – This is required to differentiate between the owner's name and the name of the business. This form is filed with the county clerk's office to prevent other individuals from securing the exact same business name.
- Business license – This is required to operate a business within a city.
- Massage license – This allows the practitioner to receive fees for massage services.
- Sales tax permit – This is required if the practitioner sells products or charges tax on services.
- Planning and zoning permits – These are required to ensure that the business meets the zoning requirements for that area, especially if the business is run out of the owner's home.
- Building safety permit – After an inspection to determine that a facility is safe for use by both employees and clients, a building permit is issued in the name of the business.
- Employers Identification Number (EIN) – This is a number assigned to the business for federal tax purposes. This is required only by partnerships and businesses that hire employees.
- Provider's number – An ID number to help identify a specific practitioner for the purposes of insurance paperwork and claims information.

Insurance

In addition to purchasing insurance to address the risks of fire and theft, the massage therapist practitioner also needs to consider other types of insurance to protect the business.
- Liability insurance covers the business in the event of any injuries on the property, or if litigation is brought against the business. If the business is run out of the home, some of these incidents may be covered under the homeowner's policy.
- Professional liability insurance guards against the possibility of litigation being brought forth by a client who feels that the practitioner caused injury or harm because they were negligent while providing services.
- Automobile insurance covers the passengers and the vehicle in the event of an accident. Coverage ranges from liability only to full coverage, regardless of fault. This insurance should be obtained as an individual, but also if a vehicle is used for business purposes and travel.
- Worker's compensation insurance covers those employees who have been hired to work for the practitioner if they become injured while on the job.
- Medical and health insurance can also be provided for the owner/practitioner and all of his employees.
- Disability insurance covers any employees who become disabled due to injuries sustained on the job.

Business ethics

In order to run a successful and ethical massage therapy practice, the massage therapist should adhere to the following guidelines to provide the best possible level of service to his or her clientele. Presenting oneself professionally, both in attitude and in appearance, and projecting a positive demeanor is important to make your clients feel at ease. Treating each client with the same level of respect, regardless of gender or age, also shows concern for the client, as does adhering to the schedule in order to provide ample time for each client. Additionally, being able to run one's business in an organized manner shows good business skills and allows the therapist to be attentive to the needs of their clients. Joining a professional organization shows the practitioner ways to increase his skills in the field, and also provides an opportunity for networking and professional growth. Finally, to perform in an ethical manner, the massage therapist should obey all the laws and legal requirements while doing business and keep his or her personal life separate from business affairs.

Marketing plan

Marketing is the process of promoting one's business with the intention of increasing income and building up the client base. Marketing generally takes the form of advertising, including written brochures, print ads in newspapers, websites, and other publications, and media ads featured on radio and television. Marketing can also take the form of referrals from repeat customers. A successful marketing plan focuses on the needs of the client and addresses how one's business can meet those needs. Marketing should be an on-going process, with adjustments made as some strategies are discovered to bring about more clientele than others. The types of marketing conducted are determined by the budget, time constraints, and also the time required for implementation. A marketing plan is an outline used by a business to determine the actions necessary to achieve a certain goal. Most marketing plans are created for a period of one to five years.

Employees

As the massage therapy practice grows, it may become necessary to add to one's staff to serve more clients. Some businesses hire massage therapists as independent contractors, while others hire them as full-time employees. As an independent contractor, the practitioner is responsible for paying his own taxes and will need to file tax forms 1099 and 1096 if he exceeds $600.00 in income during the previous year. As a full-time employee, the employer is responsible for providing an hourly paycheck and a benefits package. In either case, the person hired can help the business succeed or fail, depending on his professionalism and how personable he or she is with clients. When seeking out new employees, it is important to verify all credentials and licensing, ensure that appropriate training is provided, and work with the person to help him achieve the business's goals.

Draping

Purpose

In order to preserve a client's privacy during massage, a massage therapist will drape the client's body with linens. Besides preventing embarrassment on the part of the client, draping also keeps the client warm, which improves the efficacy of massage. When performing a full body massage, the massage therapist will have to uncover and recover body parts in order to gain access to all the necessary areas. Although the precise requirements for draping vary from state to state, as a general rule, the breasts, genitals, and gluteal cleft should remain covered at all times. The most common form of draping is known as two-sheet draping; it requires one sheet to cover the massage table and another to cover the client. Some more advanced forms of draping may require additional, smaller sheets.

Top cover method

One of the more common styles of draping is known as top cover (or two-sheet) draping. It requires the use of two large sheets: one to cover the massage table and one large enough to cover the entire client. A set of quality twin bed sheets would be suitable. In a pinch, you can use a couple of large bath towels in place of the top sheet. The patient can be wrapped in the top sheet on the way from the dressing room to the massage table. One of the benefits of a large top sheet is that you can easily lift it up to block your own view, which will allow the client to maneuver into position for the next part of the massage.

Basic techniques
At the beginning of the massage, the top cover should be positioned long-ways so that only the client's head is exposed. To massage the torso of a male, simply fold the top cover down to the waist. To massage the arms, simply fold the top cover under the client's arms at the armpits. To massage the torso of a woman, place a towel or pillowcase over the breasts and slide the cover out from under it. To massage a leg, simply slide the top cover back so that only that leg is exposed. When it is time for the client to roll over, you can either hold the cover up to block your view or hold the cover in place while the client rolls beneath it.

Full-sheet method
Some massage therapists employ the full-sheet method of draping, in which only one large sheet is used to cover both the massage table and the client. A queen-size bed sheet is usually sufficient for this kind of draping. The sheet is placed on the massage table and then folded over the client. It will be necessary to give the client a separate wrap to wear from the dressing room to the massage table. Once the client has been positioned inside the full sheet, the wrap can be removed. Some massage therapists will then take the wrap and lay it across the client's chest in order to hold the full sheet in place.

Basic techniques in full-sheet
When a client has been draped according to the full-sheet method of draping, his or her arms can be massaged by discreetly sliding them out from under the top of the sheet. When they are not exposed, the client's arms should be placed at his or her sides underneath the sheet. The legs should be undraped from the foot upwards. Otherwise, the drapes on each leg should be tucked under the legs to prevent the drape from sliding off. To massage the torso of a male, fold the top cover down to the uppermost part of the pubic bone. To massage the torso of a female, place the wrap on top of the breasts and slide the top cover out from under it while the client holds the wrap in place. When

the client needs to roll over, only cover him or her from the neck to the knees and hold the cover in place during the operation.

Communication during draping

The art of draping a client during massage is somewhat complex and may make a shy client uneasy. In order to reduce client anxiety, it is a good idea to maintain appropriate communication regarding the purpose of your draping movements. You should explain the intention of draping to every new client before beginning the massage. Before uncovering any part of the client's body, describe what you are about to do. Sometimes, you will need to hold up the sheet to block your own view as the client gets into a different position. You should always remind the client that you will not be able to see them and then describe the position you would like them to assume. Always give the client an opportunity to ask questions.

Office and equipment

Typical set-up

Depending on the extent of the practice and the funds available, the therapist should have basic equipment for the following areas of the practice: the office area, the massage area, and the restroom facility or hydrotherapy area. An independent massage therapist with a smaller practice will generally work out of their home or a small office. The business area should be cordoned off from clients for confidentiality purposes and to allow for privacy during client consultations. The restroom facility provides a place for clients to shower before and after the massage, and is also a place for the massage therapist to wash his or her hands between each massage. Finally, the massage area is made up of the massage table; a stool; a storage area for linens, oils, creams, etc.; and a dressing area for the client. Pillows or bolsters should be readily available to help make the client more comfortable during the massage. Appropriate drapes should be located nearby to give clients privacy during the massage.

Size, temperature, and furnishings

A typical massage room should be no less than 10 feet wide by 12 feet long in order to accommodate the massage table, desk, and storage areas for linens and lotions, and to provide enough space for the therapist to adequately maneuver around the table to perform the massage. Considering that the client will not have clothes on during the massage, it is important to keep the room at an ideal temperature to prevent chills. A temperature of 72° Fahrenheit would ensure the comfort of the client as well as the therapist, who may become overheated while performing the massage.

Ventilation, lighting, and music

In order to help their clients relax, massage therapists need to make some environmental adjustments to the massage room. Proper ventilation should be in place to provide fresh air that is free from odors. The lighting in the room should not be harsh and glaring; it should be reflective or soft, which will make the client feel comfortable. Purchasing dimmer switches to adjust lighting according to the client's needs and preferences would be a simple and worthwhile investment. Music also helps to promote relaxation; however, it is best to make music selections based on the client's preferences rather than the therapist's.

Massage table

Next to the massage therapist's hands, a massage table is one of the most important pieces of equipment. It should be determined whether the table will be used in a home setting or in an office environment. The table should be firm, stable, and comfortable for the client. A table that is an appropriate height is one that enables the therapist to place his hands flat on the surface while keeping his arms straight. This is the best height to provide leverage and help prevent fatigue of the back, neck, shoulders, and arms while performing the massage.

Many tables are made with hydraulic or manual height adjustments, which are especially useful if different therapists will be using the same table. The standard size of a massage table is approximately 29 inches wide by 68 to 72 inches long. This can accommodate most average-sized clients but may be too short for taller individuals. The table's padding should consist of at least one to two inches of high-density foam for optimal comfort for the client. A vinyl covering is preferred over any other type of covering, due to ease of cleaning and sanitizing between clients. To care for vinyl, a solution of mild detergent is all that is needed. Some massage tables are also adjustable to accommodate patients with different needs.

Practice Test

Practice Questions

1. Which of these is an action of the sartorius muscle?
   a. Medial rotation of the thigh
   b. Extension of the thigh
   c. Lateral rotation of the thigh
   d. Extension of the knee

2. What is the double-layered membrane that encloses the heart?
   a. Bicuspid
   b. Pericardium
   c. Endocardium
   d. Epicardium

3. Which of these conditions would be an absolute contraindication for massage?
   a. Fever
   b. Edema
   c. Pregnancy
   d. Diabetes

4. What is the result of respiration?
   a. Oxygen and carbon dioxide are exchanged between capillaries and tissue cells.
   b. Deoxygenated blood is converted to oxygenated blood.
   c. Oxygen diffuses into interstitial fluid then into tissue cells.
   d. Carbon dioxide diffuses from tissue cells into the capillaries.

5. Which technique is described as the grasping of the flesh in one or both hands and moving it up and down along the bone?
   a. Shaking
   b. Chucking
   c. Rolling
   d. Wringing

6. What is the enlarged area on the end of a long bone that articulates with another bone?
   a. Epiphysis
   b. Diaphysis
   c. Periosteum
   d. Articular cartilage

7. Which of these should be included in the preliminary assessment of a new client?
   a. Health history
   b. Height and weight measurements
   c. Resting heart rate
   d. Cholesterol check

8. Which of these lower extremity muscles does NOT have an insertion on the femur?
    a. Psoas major
    b. Tibialis anterior
    c. Adductor magnus
    d. Gluteus maximus

9. Which of these nerves would be responsible for movement of the eyeball?
    a. Trigeminal
    b. Olfactory
    c. Oculomotor
    d. Optic

10. Which of these is a characteristic of diarthrotic joints?
    a. Freely moveable
    b. Immovable
    c. Limited mobility
    d. Absence of a joint cavity

11. A client reports during the initial assessment that after shoveling snow at home that morning, there has been a consistent pain on the left side, starting at the jaw and radiating down the left arm. How should the practitioner proceed?
    a. Perform range of motion testing on the left side.
    b. Spend more time focusing on the left side during the massage.
    c. Have the client seek immediate medical attention.
    d. Avoid the left side during the massage.

12. Which of these massage techniques is applied in a transverse direction to the tissue being treated?
    a. Effleurage
    b. Petrissage
    c. Cross-fiber friction
    d. Chucking

13. What would be the appropriate adjustment to the massage session if a client reports current use of painkillers?
    a. Increase the depth of the strokes so that the client can better feel the massage
    b. Increase the depth of the strokes to prevent tissue damage because sensation may be dulled.
    c. No change to the massage session would be necessary.
    d. Refuse treatment for this client.

14. Which of these techniques would be used to desensitize a nerve?
    a. Wringing
    b. Shaking
    c. Effleurage
    d. Vibration

15. Why must caution be used when treating a client on blood-thinning medication?
    a. The client may not be sensitive to pressure.
    b. There is increased risk of bruising.
    c. There is increased risk of muscle spasm.
    d. The client's blood sugar may be high.

16. What is the longest part of the alimentary canal that is lined with small, fingerlike projections called villi?
    a. Small intestine
    b. Large intestine
    c. Digestive tract
    d. Esophagus

17. The cubital area of the elbow is an endangerment site. Which of these nerves pass through that area and should be avoided?
    a. Sciatic nerve
    b. Tibial nerve
    c. Optic nerve
    d. Median nerve

18. What is the smallest functional unit of a muscle cell?
    a. Actin
    b. Myosin
    c. Sarcomere
    d. Spindle

19. Which of these conditions is the accumulation of interstitial fluid in the soft tissue that is caused by blockage, inflammation, or removal of the lymph channels?
    a. Hematoma
    b. Cancer
    c. Lymphedema
    d. Phlebitis

20. Which of these conditions involves the inflammation of veins accompanied by pain and swelling?
    a. Aneurysm
    b. Phlebitis
    c. Lymphedema
    d. Myocardial infarction

21. What is the effect of light percussion on the blood vessels?
    a. Dilation followed by contraction
    b. Contraction followed by relaxation as movement continues
    c. Continuous contraction until the movement stops
    d. Increased permeability of the vessels

22. Which of these techniques would be applied with the ulnar side of the hand?
    a. Tapping
    b. Jostling
    c. Slapping
    d. Hacking

23. Where are the adrenal glands located?
    a. On the pancreas
    b. On either side of the trachea
    c. On top of each kidney
    d. Behind the thyroid

24. In this type of deep palpation, the tissues are palpated perpendicular to the surface.
    a. Shear
    b. Compression
    c. Superficial
    d. Subcutaneous

25. Which type of muscle contraction results in the distance between the ends of the muscle becoming shorter?
    a. Isotonic contraction
    b. Isometric contraction
    c. Fast-twitch contraction
    d. Slow-twitch contraction

26. When all of the internal systems of the body are in balance, what is this is known as?
    a. Homeopathy
    b. Gate theory
    c. Hyperemia
    d. Homeostasis

27. Which endangerment site is bordered by the sternocleidomastoid and trapezius muscles and the clavicle?
    a. Femoral triangle
    b. Anterior triangle of the neck
    c. Posterior triangle of the neck
    d. Popliteal fossa

28. Which of these is NOT a factor in determining scope of practice?
    a. Activities that are legally acceptable according to the licenses of the profession
    b. The age and sex of the practitioner
    c. Training received by the practitioner
    d. Choice of preferred clientele

29. Which of these would NOT be a benefit of massage to the critically ill?
    a. Decreases pain receptors
    b. Reduces disorientation
    c. Reduces isolation
    d. Improves mobility

30. Which of these massage techniques would be stimulating to the nervous system?
    a. Gentle stroking
    b. Light friction
    c. Vibration
    d. Ischemic compression

31. What is the benefit of ischemic compression?
    a. Increases adrenaline
    b. Stimulates the peripheral nerves
    c. Releases the reflex cycle that maintains hypertension in the muscle
    d. Increases lymph flow to the extremities

32. Which of the following would be considered an open-ended question?
    a. Do you smoke?
    b. Do you have a referral from a physician?
    c. How would you describe your current pain level?
    d. Have you had a surgery in the past?

33. Which of these is NOT a principal function of the skin?
    a. Protection
    b. Heat regulation
    c. Absorption
    d. Regrowth

34. A vertical plumb line running from above the head along the lateral side of the body to the floor, when viewed from the side, would pass through which of these structures?
    a. Pubic symphysis
    b. Iliac crest
    c. Acromioclavicular joint
    d. Acetabulum

35. Which of these muscles has an attachment site on the clavicle?
    a. Levator scapulae
    b. Pectoralis major
    c. Pectoralis minor
    d. Teres major

36. During a visual assessment, the practitioner observes that the client's right shoulder is elevated. Which of the following muscles is most likely involved?
    a. Levator scapulae
    b. Pectoralis minor
    c. Lower trapezius
    d. Rhomboid major

37. What is an acute inflammation caused by the herpes zoster virus that creates inflammation at a nerve trunk and the dendrites at the end of the sensory neurons called?
    a. Neuritis
    b. Polio
    c. Meningitis
    d. Shingles

38. While palpating the neck the practitioner may feel these small nodules, which are between the size of a pea and a kidney bean.
    a. Pineal glands
    b. Ganglia
    c. Lymph nodes
    d. Facet joints

39. Which of these is an effect of increased serotonin levels?
    a. An increase in feelings of stress
    b. An increase in food cravings
    c. A higher incidence of eating disorders
    d. An increase in feelings of calm and well-being

40. What is the bony prominence that can be palpated at the hip joint?
    a. Greater tubercle
    b. Greater trochanter
    c. Acromion
    d. Femoral tuberosity

41. Which of these would be considered a form of nonverbal communication?
    a. Sighing
    b. Frowning
    c. Whispering
    d. Questioning

42. Which of these types of barriers is the first sign of resistance to a movement?
    a. Anatomic barrier
    b. Physiologic barrier
    c. End barrier
    d. Resistive barrier

43. A client is two months post-surgery and cleared for massage. Which of these techniques would be most effective for aligning the scar tissue at the surgical site?
    a. Tapping
    b. Cross-fiber friction
    c. Petrissage
    d. Vibration

44. What is the largest lymph vessel of the body?
    a. Cervical lymph nodes
    b. Thoracic duct
    c. Spleen
    d. Internal jugular

45. What is a form of energetic manipulation often used in hospitals by nurses?
    a. Neuromuscular therapy
    b. Myofascial release
    c. Therapeutic touch
    d. Alexander technique

46. What is the purpose of Golgi tendon organs?
    a. To sense the movement and position of joints
    b. To activate muscle contraction
    c. To maintain balance
    d. To measure the amount of tension in a muscle due to stretching and contracting

47. What is a set of guiding moral principles that directs a person's choice of actions and behaviors?
    a. Professional boundary
    b. Therapeutic relationship
    c. Code of ethics
    d. Ethical arrangement

48. Why is massage in the supine position for more than ten to fifteen minutes not recommended after the twentieth week of pregnancy?
    a. The uterus can put pressure on the major lymph and blood vessels of the abdomen.
    b. The ligaments and joints are too loose to maintain the position.
    c. There will be too much pressure on the lungs.
    d. It tends to make the fetus very active.

49. Which of these would NOT be a way for a practitioner to maintain appropriate interpersonal space with a client before and after the massage?
    a. Carry on conversations at eye level.
    b. Remain standing while the client is seated.
    c. Complete most of the important conversation before the client is on the table.
    d. Maintain a comfortable distance from the client while talking.

50. Which of these hormones causes acceleration in heart rate and inhibition of the digestive system?
    a. Epinephrine
    b. Dopamine
    c. Estrogen
    d. Melatonin

51. A client comments during the massage that a coworker is also receiving massage from the practitioner and enquires about the coworker's condition. How should the practitioner respond?
    a. The practitioner should inform the client that it is against confidentiality guidelines to share personal information.
    b. The practitioner should give a brief summary of the client's condition without divulging too much information.
    c. The practitioner should encourage the client to talk to his or her coworker about the condition.
    d. The practitioner should ask the client if the coworker has reported satisfactory progress from the massage.

52. What is it called when a client gives written authorization for professional services based on the client's full understanding of the expectations, benefits, and any undesirable effects?
    a. A treatment plan
    b. Explanation of benefits
    c. Informed consent
    d. Consultation

53. Which of these would be a code of ethics violation according to the National Certification Board for Therapeutic Massage and Bodywork's Code of Ethics?
    a. Refuse to treat a client because the practitioner does not feel competent to treat the client's condition.
    b. Provide treatment only when there is a reasonable expectation that it would be advantageous to the client.
    c. Attend continuing education.
    d. Accept gifts from a client who has had extraordinary results from treatment.

54. A client complains of lower back pain during the massage. Where is this information documented on a SOAP chart?
    a. Objective
    b. Subjective
    c. Assessment or applications
    d. Planning

55. A client invites the practitioner out for drinks with friends after the massage. How should the practitioner respond?
    a. The practitioner should ask where and what time.
    b. The practitioner should suggest a meal before drinks.
    c. The practitioner should tell the client that drinking after massage is not recommended.
    d. The practitioner should gently inform the client that personal relationships outside of the massage setting are not appropriate.

56. What is a Japanese finger pressure technique that affects the circulation of fluids and chi?
    a. Reiki
    b. Shiatsu
    c. Ayurveda
    d. Anatripsis

57. Slow, rhythmic massage of which of these areas can elicit a sexual response?
    a. Lower back
    b. Feet
    c. Lower abdomen
    d. Hands

58. What is the definition of the word *anatripsis*?
    a. Rubbing of the head to relieve headache
    b. The lifting and grasping of the tissues to make space between the tissues
    c. The art of rubbing a part upward, not downward
    d. The rubbing of the limbs to strengthen the muscles and combat paralysis

59. Which form should be signed by the client to provide an update of status to the client's physician?
    a. Health history form
    b. Release of information form
    c. HIPAA form
    d. SOAP chart

60. Which of these is a stance where the practitioner stands with both feet in line with the edge of the table and moves by shifting the weight side to side?
    a. Archer stance
    b. Horse stance
    c. Saddle stance
    d. Grounding stance

61. Which of these is NOT a characteristic of licensing?
    a. Is issued by a governmental agency
    b. Is voluntary to show proficiency or accomplishment
    c. Specifies a scope of practice
    d. Determines minimum requirements for compliance

62. Which of these types of muscles is involuntary, nonstriated, and can maintain a contraction for a long period of time?
    a. Smooth muscle
    b. Cardiac muscle
    c. Skeletal muscle
    d. Fast twitch muscle

63. Which of these would be a reason for a license to be revoked, suspended, or canceled?
    a. Accepting a large tip from a client
    b. Asking a client about his or her divorce
    c. Prescribing drugs
    d. Practicing new massage techniques on a client

64. Which of these would be classified as a synarthrotic joint?
    a. Sutures of the skull
    b. Sacroiliac joint
    c. Hip joint
    d. Shoulder joint

65. What are personal comfort zones that help a person maintain a feeling of comfort and safety?
    a. Boundaries
    b. Ethics
    c. Morals
    d. Values

66. What accommodations should a massage practitioner make when working with a frail, elderly client?
    a. No accommodations need to be made as long as the client is healthy.
    b. Require the client to have a friend or family member assist them onto the table.
    c. Use a lighter touch because the tissues are more delicate and susceptible to bruising.
    d. Frail, elderly clients should not receive massage.

67. How can a practitioner set boundaries related to time?
    a. Always finish the massage early so the next appointment can start on time.
    b. Set policies regarding no shows and late arrivals.
    c. Tell clients that the appointment time is fifteen minutes before the scheduled time to ensure early arrival.
    d. Don't schedule appointments after 7:00 pm.

68. According to this theory, stimulation of thermo- or mechanoreceptors using massage, ice, or rubbing will suppress pain sensations where the fibers enter the spinal column.
    a. Pain control theory
    b. Mechanical control theory
    c. Gate control theory
    d. Sensory control theory

69. What is the ideal temperature range for the massage room?
    a. 68 to 72 degrees Fahrenheit
    b. 72 to 75 degrees Fahrenheit
    c. 76 to 80 degrees Fahrenheit
    d. 62 to 66 degrees Fahrenheit

70. Which of these is NOT a goal of the initial consultation?
    a. Establish open communication with the client
    b. Perform a preliminary assessment
    c. Obtain informed consent
    d. Palpate for muscular imbalances

71. The practitioner begins to cough excessively during the massage. What is the appropriate course of action?
    a. Cough in to the sleeve and continue the massage.
    b. Apologize for being so loud.
    c. Apologize and leave the room to get water and wash hands thoroughly before returning.
    d. Offer the client a discount.

72. In which section of a SOAP chart should the results of range of motion testing be recorded?
    a. Objective
    b. Subjective
    c. Assessment or applications
    d. Planning

73. What is the system of infection control created to protect persons from blood and blood borne pathogens?
    a. Universal precautions
    b. Sterilization
    c. Disinfecting
    d. Safety protocol

74. Who made gymnastics and the regular use of massage part of their physical fitness rituals?
    a. Greeks
    b. Japanese
    c. Chinese
    d. Hindu

75. What is the proper bleach-to-water solution ratio for disinfecting surfaces?
    a. 1:5
    b. 1:100
    c. 1:20
    d. 1:10

76. Which of these is NOT an endangerment site?
    a. Medial brachium
    b. Popliteal fossa
    c. Upper lumbar area
    d. Quadriceps triangle

77. Which of the following would be a reason for the practitioner to wear vinyl gloves during the massage?
    a. When the client has soiled feet
    b. When the practitioner has sweaty hands
    c. When the practitioner has an open wound on the hand
    d. When the client has a fever

78. What is the term for when a practitioner develops strong emotional feelings toward a client?
    a. Countertransference
    b. Transference
    c. Dual relationship
    d. Abusive

79. How can a practitioner use leverage to apply deeper pressure without using muscle strength from the hands and arms?
    a. Climb onto the table.
    b. Use the elbows.
    c. Stand on the toes.
    d. Lean into the technique.

80. What are the rights and activities that are legally acceptable under the license of a particular profession defined by?
   a. Code of ethics
   b. Certification
   c. Local ordinance
   d. Scope of practice

81. Where is the proper position for a bolster when the client is lying on the table in the supine position?
   a. Behind the knees
   b. Under the ankles
   c. Under the lower back
   d. None at all

82. Which of these types of neurons carries a signal indicating pain from a sense organ to the brain?
   a. Efferent neurons
   b. Interneurons
   c. Neurotransmitter
   d. Afferent neurons

83. How can a practitioner secure the draping while the client is rolling over?
   a. Lift the sheet off of the table.
   b. Ask the client to hold onto the drape while rolling over.
   c. Use an extra-long sheet on top.
   d. Lean on the table.

84. Which of the following would NOT be an inert tissue?
   a. Bursa
   b. Nerve
   c. Ligament
   d. Tendon

85. What is a short, general statement that defines the main focus of a business?
   a. Mission statement
   b. Business plan
   c. Purpose
   d. Strategic plan

86. A new client reports during the initial interview that there has been a recent diagnosis of cancer and treatments have not yet begun. How should the massage practitioner continue?
   a. The practitioner should request a doctor's recommendation before treating the client.
   b. The practitioner should perform a full-body massage and avoid the area of the body that is affected by the cancer.
   c. The practitioner should call the treating physician's office and ask for permission to treat the client.
   d. The practitioner should refer the client to another massage practitioner who has experience treating cancer patients.

87. Which of these would be a characteristic of being an independent contractor, according to the Internal Revenue Service?
    a. Receiving vacation days
    b. Hours of work set by the business owner
    c. Freedom to set own hours
    d. Taxes withheld from the paycheck

88. Which of these would NOT be a benefit of massage to a person with cancer?
    a. Increases blood flow to tumor site
    b. Boosts the healing process
    c. Reduces edema
    d. Improves flow of lymph

89. What is a business setup that is subject to regulation and taxation and requires a charter?
    a. Sole proprietorship
    b. Corporation
    c. Partnership
    d. Limited liability company

90. Which of the following is NOT an inert tissue?
    a. Tendon
    b. Ligament
    c. Bursa
    d. Nerve

91. Which organ of the digestive system contains glands that produce hydrochloric acid?
    a. Gallbladder
    b. Stomach
    c. Pancreas
    d. Large Intestine

92. Which of these advanced massage modalities most addresses trigger points and their relationship to local and referred pain?
    a. Myofascial release
    b. Therapeutic touch
    c. Muscle energy technique
    d. Neuromuscular therapy

93. What is the origin of the anterior fibers of the deltoid muscle?
    a. Lateral one-third of the clavicle
    b. Lesser tubercle of the humerus
    c. Costal cartilage of ribs one through six
    d. Deltoid tuberosity of the humerus

94. Which plexus of the nervous system provides e supply to the abdominal organs?
    a. Brachial plexus
    b. Cervical plexus
    c. Lumbar plexus
    d. Sacral plexus

95. Which of these is an example of a dual relationship?
    a. When a client is referred to the massage practitioner by a physician
    b. When the practitioner refers the client to another massage practitioner
    c. When the client is requesting massage for more than one condition
    d. When the client and practitioner belong to the same social organization

96. What is the muscle that performs the opposite movement of the prime mover?
    a. Fixator
    b. Agonist
    c. Antagonist
    d. Synergist

97. What are the three types of end feels that are considered normal?
    a. Hard, soft, springy
    b. Springy, empty, hard
    c. Soft, empty, short
    d. Hard, inert, springy

98. Which of the following drugs is classified as a non-opioid analgesic?
    a. Percocet
    b. Morphine
    c. Demerol
    d. Tylenol

99. What is the term for when a client attempts to personalize the relationship with the massage practitioner by projecting characteristics of someone from a previous relationship?
    a. Countertransference
    b. Duality
    c. Transference
    d. Therapeutic

100. A client is being seen for muscular tightness in the low back that has been evaluated by a physician. The physician referred the client for massage after finding no injury. The client reports that after six massage sessions, there has been no change in symptoms. How should the practitioner proceed?
    a. The practitioner should reassess the client to evaluate whether a change in treatment is justified.
    b. The practitioner should proceed with the massage as stated in the treatment plan.
    c. The practitioner should refuse treatment to the client.
    d. The practitioner should refer the client to another physician.

Answers and Explanations

1. C: The sartorius muscle has multiple actions. It flexes, laterally rotates, abducts the thigh, and assists with flexion and medial rotation of the knee.

2. B: The pericardium is the double-layered membrane that encloses the heart. It is made up of two layers, a thin inner layer, which provides a serous covering for the heart, and an outer layer made up of fibrous connective tissue, which serves as protection.

3. A: Massage is contraindicated when fever is present. Normal body temperature is 98.6 degrees Fahrenheit. If the client feels abnormally warm, the temperature should be taken. Most physicians and therapists will advise against massage when the body temperature is above 99.4 degrees Fahrenheit. Fever is the body's natural defense system against an invading pathogen. Massage could disrupt this natural process.

4. B: External respiration happens in the lungs. It is when deoxygenated blood that is coming from the right side of the heart is oxygenated and returned to the left side of the heart. It is an exchange of oxygen and carbon dioxide between the air in the alveoli of the lungs and the blood of the pulmonary capillaries.

5. B: Chucking is a technique that is described as the grasping of flesh in one or both hands and moving it up and down along the bone. It is performed as a series of quick movements along the axis of the bone. It is considered a friction movement.

6. A: A long bone has an enlarged area on each end, the epiphysis, which serves as an articulation point for other bones. The epiphysis is covered with a layer of hyaline cartilage known as the articular cartilage. This provides a smooth surface for the two bones to form a joint. The articular cartilage also provides a shock-absorbing surface for the articulation.

7. A: In the preliminary assessment the massage practitioner needs to understand as much about the client as possible. Depending on the type of massage being offered, the assessment may be more superficial or more in depth. The practitioner should always be sure to take a thorough health history of the client to be aware of any contraindications or cautions to make an informed decision regarding the treatment plan.

8. B: The tibialis anterior does not have an attachment on the femur. This muscle originates at the lateral and proximal one half of the tibia and the interosseous membrane and inserts in to the medial and plantar surface of the medial cuneiform and the base of the first metatarsal.

9. C: The oculomotor nerve is the third cranial nerve. It controls the movement of the eyelid and the eyeball and causes constriction of the pupil. It originates in the midbrain and passes through the superior orbital fissure. It is considered primarily a motor nerve.

10. A: Diarthrotic joints are freely moveable joints. These joints have an articular cartilage and are surrounded by a joint capsule that contains synovial fluid that lubricates the joint surfaces. They are capable of different kinds of movements. Some examples of diarthrotic joints are pivot joints, hinge joints, ball and socket joints, and saddle joints.

11. C: If a client reports pain in the left arm, this can be a sign of a heart attack. Pain radiating down from the jaw on to the left side is often an early sign of heart attack. Shoveling snow is a very common cause of heart attack, especially in those who are sedentary. Someone demonstrating these symptoms should seek medical attention immediately to rule out a heart-related condition. Other signs of heart attack would be shortness of breath, lightheadedness, and chest pain.

12. C: Cross-fiber friction is applied in a transverse direction with the tips of the fingers or the thumb. It is applied across the fibers of muscle, tendon, or ligament with the intent to break up adhesions and scar tissue, align the fibers, and broaden and separate the tissue.

13. B: If a client reports current use of painkillers, the practitioner should decrease the depth of the strokes to prevent tissue damage because sensation may be dulled and tissue response may not be normal. The client may not be able to accurately report the proper pressure tolerance after taking painkillers. It is recommended that the client receive massage at the end of the dosage regimen so that pain information is more accurate.

14. D: Vibration is a technique that can be done manually or with an electronic device. When vibrations are applied for a prolonged period it has an anesthetizing effect. It is often used to desensitize nerves or areas of the body.

15. B: Blood thinners or anticoagulants such as Heparin and Warfarin are used to prevent blood from clotting. Caution must be used on clients who are taking blood thinners. The risk of bruising or internal bleeding is increased, especially in the elderly.

16. A: The small intestine is part of the digestive system and is the longest part of the alimentary canal. The small intestine contains three parts: the duodenum, jejunum, and ileum. Villi are the small, fingerlike projections that increase the surface area of the small intestine and allow for greater absorption.

17. D: The cubital area is the anterior bend of the elbow. It is an endangerment site because the median nerve, radial and ulnar arteries, and median cubital vein pass through this area. These can be easily compressed if deep manipulations or direct sustained pressure occurs at this site.

18. C: The smallest functional unit of a muscle cell is the sarcomere. Inside each sarcomere are the proteins myosin and actin. The myosin and actin line up to create the striated appearance of skeletal muscle. The activity of the actin and myosin filaments in the sarcomere is what gives muscle its contractile ability.

19. C: Lymphedema is a swelling that occurs when interstitial fluid accumulates in the soft tissue, usually in the extremities. The fluid is unable to pass due a blockage, inflammation, or removal of lymph channels. It can be caused by surgery, trauma, radiation, or infection. It can also occur due to a congenital or genetic condition that prevents the lymph system from developing completely.

20. B: Phlebitis is the inflammation of veins that is accompanied by pain and swelling. It can be caused by infection, injury, or surgery or have no known cause. A blood clot can form along the inflamed vein and develop into a condition known as deep vein thrombosis (DVT).

21. B: Light percussion strokes will initially cause the blood vessels to contract, but with continued movement there will be a relaxation of the blood vessels.

22. D: Hacking is a rapid striking movement that is done with the little finger and the ulnar side of the hand. It can be performed with one or both hands. The wrist and fingers should remain loose and relaxed with the fingers spread apart slightly. The fingers will come together as the hand strikes the body, causing a vibratory effect.

23. C: The adrenal glands are located on the top of each kidney and are made of up two parts, the medulla and the adrenal cortex. The medulla produces epinephrine and norepinephrine. The adrenal cortex produces corticosteroids.

24. B: Compression is a form of deep palpation. The tissue is palpated through layers perpendicular to the surface. Compression is often used to palpate muscle and its associated structures.

25. A: A muscle contraction that results in the distance between the ends of the muscle becoming shorter is an isotonic contraction. When the distance between the ends of the muscle becomes shorter, this is known as a concentric isotonic contraction. The opposite contraction, when the distance between the ends of the muscle becomes longer, is known as an eccentric isotonic contraction. All isotonic contractions cause changes in the distance between the ends of a muscle.

26. D: Homeostasis is the body's natural internal balance. It is maintained by the work of both the sympathetic and parasympathetic nervous systems. The body strives to remain in a state of homeostasis.

27. C: The posterior triangle of the neck is an endangerment site on the body that is bordered by the sternocleidomastoid muscle, the trapezius muscle, and the clavicle. It contains the brachial plexus, the subclavian artery, the brachiocephalic vein, the external jugular vein, and lymph nodes. All of these are structures of concern, and caution must be used when massaging in this area.

28. B: The scope of practice is determined by what is legally acceptable under the license of the practitioner. Factors that also influence a practitioner's scope of practice are the skills and interests of the practitioner, the training received, and the type of clientele the practitioner would like to work with.

29. A: Massage has no effect on the number of pain receptors in the body. It can help those who are critically ill by reducing disorientation and isolation and improving mobility. Massage also helps with discomfort and pain and eases emotional strain.

30. C: Vibration movements such as shaking and trembling will stimulate the peripheral nerves and all nerve centers associated with a specific nerve trunk.

31. C: Ischemic compression or, holding of pressure, on a sensitive trigger point can release the reflex cycle that is maintaining hypertension in a muscle. It does this by desensitizing the trigger point, which stops the pathophysiological reflex cycle from continuing.

32. C: When questioning a client regarding current concerns and any health issues that are present, the practitioner should ask open-ended questions. Open-ended questions are ones that cannot be answered with a simple yes or no and require further explanation. This allows the practitioner to better understand the client's needs and health situation.

33. D: The principal functions of the skin are: protection, heat regulation, secretion and excretion, sensation, absorption, and respiration.

34. D: A vertical plumb line that runs from the head to the floor when viewed from the side should pass through the ear, shoulder, elbow, acetabulum, knee, and just in front of the ankle. This plumb line can be used to detect postural deviations or abnormalities in clients as part of the assessment process.

35. B: The pectoralis major has two heads, the clavicular and sternal. The clavicular head originates at the clavicle and inserts into the lateral ridge of the bicipital groove of the humerus. The sternal head originates at the sternum and costal cartilages of ribs one through six and inserts into the lateral ridge of the bicipital groove of the humerus.

36. A: The levator scapulae muscle originates on the transverse processes of C1–C4 and inserts into the superior one-third of the vertebral border of the scapula. The actions of the levator scapulae are elevation of the scapula and lateral flexion of the neck. If this muscle is hypertonic, it can hold the scapula in an elevated position and would be visible upon observation.

37. D: Shingles is an acute inflammation caused by the herpes zoster virus. It causes inflammation of a nerve trunk and the dendrites at the end of sensory neurons. Shingles presents as a rash with water blisters that appears in a confined area on one side of the body. The rash will seldom cross the midline. The virus causes a band of pain that follows the dermatomes of the body. Massage is contraindicated due to pain and risk of infection.

38. C: Lymph nodes can be palpated on the sides of the neck, in the axillary region, or in the inguinal area. They are small nodules between the size of a pea and a kidney bean. At times they can be enlarged due to illness. If a practitioner palpates enlarged lymph nodes, it should be brought to the attention of the client.

39. D: Serotonin is a neurotransmitter. It has many influences on the body including affecting mood, behavior, appetite, blood pressure, temperature regulation, memory, and learning ability. It counters the effects of norepinephrine, promotes a sense of calm and well-being, suppresses irritability, and reduces cravings for food and sex.

40. B: The greater trochanter is the bony knob at the top of the femur. It can be easily palpated at the hip. It is an attachment site for many muscles, including the gluteus maximus and the lateral rotators of the hip.

41. B: Frowning is a form of nonverbal communication. Nonverbal communication is posturing, gestures, and facial expressions that express a person's mental, emotional, or physical state. It is important for a massage practitioner to observe these nonverbal clues as well as verbal feedback from the client.

42. D: The first sign of resistance to a movement is the resistive barrier. It is well within the anatomical limits of the involved tissues. It is the bind felt when the contractile tissue is reaching the outer limits of its range of motion. Incremental force can be used to move past this barrier and on to the physiologic and anatomic barriers.

43. B: Cross-fiber friction is applied using the tips of the fingers or the thumb directly to the site of a lesion or scar. It is applied in a transverse direction to the fibers. The intent of cross-fiber friction is to align fibrous tissue, break up adhesions, and soften scar tissue.

44. B: The thoracic duct, also known as the left lymphatic duct, is the largest lymphatic vessel of the body. It collects lymph from the legs, abdomen, left arm, and left side of the head, neck, and chest. The lymph from the thoracic duct reenters the bloodstream at the left subclavian vein and from there flows to the heart.

45. C: Therapeutic touch is a simple form of bodywork that is very popular with nurses. It is based on the belief that all people have the inherent ability to heal and that anyone can be a vessel for healing. The purpose is to balance the energy fields and aura of the body by contacting them with the hands held above and off of the body.

46. D: Golgi tendon organs can be found at the musculotendinous junction, where tendons attach to muscle fibers. They are sensory nerve organs that sense the amount of tension in the muscle cells due to the stretching and contracting of the muscle. They also measure the amount of force on the bone at the tendon attachment.

47. C: A profession is generally represented by a professional association regulated and guided by a code of ethics. A code of ethics is a set of moral principles that direct the professional's choice of actions. Both the National Certification Board for Therapeutic Massage and Bodywork and the American Massage Therapy Association have codes of ethics that guide massage practitioners toward making ethical and professional choices.

48. A: After the twentieth week of pregnancy, massage longer than ten to fifteen minutes should be avoided in the supine position due to the increasing size of the uterus, which can put pressure on the major lymph and blood vessels of the abdomen. Safer positioning, such as a semi-reclining position, which places the torso at an elevated forty-five- to seventy-degree angle is recommended. A small bolster could be placed under the right shoulder and hip during supine massage to give a left lateral tilt to the uterus, which will prevent it from placing pressure on the abdominal vena cava and aorta.

49. B: Interpersonal space is the physical space maintained between the client and practitioner before and after the massage. This space should make both parties comfortable. It is important to respect the height and power differential while maintaining personal space. It is best that conversations are held at eye level whenever possible. Both parties should either sit or stand while speaking. When one party is much taller of if one party is seated while the other party stands, this gives a sense of power to the person at a greater height.

50. A: Epinephrine is the body's fight-or-flight hormone. Epinephrine is secreted by the adrenal glands to prepare the body to respond to stress or emergencies. It accelerates the heart rate and activates sweat glands. The blood flow is diverted away from digestion and toward the muscles, which inhibits digestion and prepares the body for activity.

51. A: Maintaining client confidentiality is extremely important. The practitioner must never divulge information about another client without that client's permission in writing. Any time that an enquiry is made about another client, no matter the relationship, the practitioner must inform that person that it is against confidentiality guidelines to share personal information about a current or former client.

52. C: Informed consent is the process of the practitioner providing enough information to the client so that the client is able to fully understand the nature and extent of the massage services being offered. The client is given disclosure of the services, policies, and procedures as well as

information on benefits and side effects. With this information, the client is able to give informed consent to proceed with treatment. It is recommended that the client sign an informed consent form before receiving massage.

53. D: According to the code of ethics of the National Certification Board for Therapeutic Massage and Bodywork, a massage practitioner should "refuse any gifts or benefits that are intended to influence a referral, decision, or treatment or that are purely for personal gain and not for the good of the client." A client may show appreciation by giving a tip to the practitioner, as is customary, but gifts should not be accepted.

54. B: The subjective, or S, section of a SOAP chart is where the client's reporting of symptoms, aggravating or relieving activities, and pain levels are documented. This is not measurable or observable data but the subjective reporting of the client. Also included in this section would be the client's experiences, expectations, and goals.

55. D: If a client asks the practitioner to participate in social activities outside of the massage setting, the practitioner should gently turn down the request. It is important to maintain professional and personal boundaries with a client. Socializing with a client could lead to more serious ethical violations and disrupt the therapeutic relationship.

56. B: The Japanese massage technique known as Shiatsu is used to affect the circulation of fluids and chi. Finger pressure is used to stimulate nerves that are aligned to the Chinese pressure points used in acupressure. These points are believed to increase the flow of fluids and the life force, known as chi, throughout the body.

57. C: Any time that a practitioner provides slow, rhythmic massage in the lower abdomen area, as well as the buttocks and thighs, it is possible to elicit a sexual response in the client. A sexual response can be easily recognized as a penile erection in males. In women it is not as obvious but can be demonstrated by flushing of the skin and fidgeting.

58. C: Anatripsis is the rubbing of a part upward, not downward. This word was used by Hippocrates in his writings on massage.

59. B: Under HIPAA laws created in 2001, a health practitioner who stores or transmits personal health information electronically must not divulge any client information to a third party without first obtaining a written release of information form that is signed by the client. Massage practitioners may not be required to be HIPAA compliant but should always strive to maintain the highest level of confidentiality for clients.

60. B: The horse stance is used most often when kneading the back and the legs. The practitioner's feet are in line with the edge of the table, and movement is applied by shifting the weight from side to side. The practitioner can lean into the client for deeper pressure. In this posture the back should be relaxed and erect with the shoulders dropped down and back.

61. B: Licensing is a requirement for conducting a business or practicing a particular trade or craft. A license is issued by a regulating agency of the state or municipality. It sets the minimum requirements for compliance in that profession, specifies a scope of practice, and must be renewed at predetermined intervals.

62. A: Smooth muscle is involuntary and controlled by the autonomic nervous system. The cells are nonstriated and spindle shaped and will commonly form fibrous bands. Smooth muscle is found in the stomach, intestines, and blood vessels. It does not attach to bone, can hold a contraction for a long time, and will not easily fatigue.

63. C: Prescribing drugs would be a reason for a license to be revoked, suspended, or canceled. Other reasons for license suspension, cancellation, or revocation would be fraud in obtaining the license, being convicted of a felony, acts of prostitution, practicing under a false or assumed name, being addicted to narcotics or alcohol, being negligent in the practice of massage, ethical or sexual misconduct, and practicing beyond the scope permitted by law.

64. A: The sutures of the skull are classified as synarthrotic joints. A synarthrotic joint is one that is classified as essentially immovable. This is the functional classification of a joint. Joints can also be classified according to their structure.

65. A: Boundaries are a way for a person to maintain a feeling of comfort and safety. They are personal comfort zones that can be professional, personal, physical, emotional, intellectual, or sexual. To have a healthy therapeutic relationship with a client, a practitioner must understand and respect personal and professional boundaries.

66. C: The tissue of the frail elderly is delicate and more susceptible to bruising. Care must be taken when massaging elderly or frail clients. Many times the skin is paper thin and is easily damaged. A lighter touch is recommended.

67. B: It is important for a massage practitioner to set clear professional boundaries related to time. The practitioner should set clear policies regarding no shows and late arrivals so that the client understands the boundaries and knows what to expect regarding scheduling and arriving on time for the massage.

68. C: Gate control theory states that impulses of pain are transmitted from the nociceptors to the brain via both small- and large-diameter nerve fibers. Stimulation of thermo- or mechanoreceptors is transmitted via large-diameter fibers only. When thermo- or mechanoreceptors are stimulated through massage, ice, or rubbing, those sensations suppress the pain sensations at the gate where the fibers enter the spinal column, thus blocking those sensations from being sent to the brain.

69. B: The ideal temperature for a massage room is 72 to 75 degrees Fahrenheit. This temperature will prevent the client from becoming too cold while on the table and also prevent the practitioner from becoming too warm while performing the massage.

70. D: During the initial consultation with a client, the goals of the practitioner should include establishing a rapport with the client, explaining policies and procedures, determining the needs and expectations of the client, reviewing the health history and intake forms, performing a preliminary assessment, formulating a treatment plan, and obtaining informed consent. Palpation for muscular imbalances would be a part of the ongoing assessment process that happens during the massage.

71. C: If the massage practitioner begins to cough excessively during the massage, the practitioner should apologize to the client for the disruption and leave the room to get water to quiet the cough. Once the coughing has subsided, the practitioner should wash hands thoroughly and return to the room.

72. A: In the objective, or O, section of a SOAP chart, the practitioner reports information that is gathered from observation, interviewing, and assessment tests. This information should be measurable data or the observations of the practitioner. The practitioner's treatment goals should also be included in this section.

73. A: Universal precautions are a system of infection control created to protect persons from blood and blood-borne pathogens. It assumes that all blood and bodily fluids are potentially infectious from diseases such as HIV and hepatitis. It lays out the specific procedures for handling bodily fluids and cleaning linens and surfaces that have come in contact with blood and other bodily fluids.

74. A: The Greeks were the first to combine the modalities of exercise and massage and were the founders of the first gymnasium. Gymnasiums were where physical fitness rituals using massage and exercise were performed. The gymnasiums were an important part of Greek life and served as centers where scholars, athletes, soldiers, and the sick came to be treated for disease and to promote health.

75. D: Chlorine bleach is an effective disinfectant for surfaces, implements, and linens. For surfaces and implements, a 1:10 solution should be prepared. Combine one part bleach to nine parts water. Implements should be immersed in the solution for ten minutes. For linens one cup bleach can be added to hot water during the wash cycle.

76. D: The medial brachium, popliteal fossa, and upper lumbar are all endangerment sites on the body. These areas all have major nerves, blood vessels, or vital organs that are exposed. Deep manipulation or direct, sustained pressure should be avoided in these areas.

77. C: A practitioner should wear vinyl gloves or another appropriate type of coverage anytime there is broken skin or any type of infection on the hands. This is to protect both the client and practitioner.

78. A: When a practitioner begins to personalize the therapeutic relationship with a client, this is known as countertransference. Signs of countertransference are strong emotional feelings toward the client, thinking excessively about a client between sessions, wearing special clothing when a certain client is coming, spending extra time with a client, having sexual feelings about a client, having feelings of dread about upcoming appointments with a certain client, or having negative reactions to a client.

79. D: To apply deeper pressure without using muscle strength from the hands and arms, a massage practitioner can use leverage by leaning into the technique. The practitioner, as a general rule, should stay behind the area being worked on instead of in front of it. This will allow for better leverage and body alignment.

80. D: Scope of practice is the set of rights and activities that have been defined as legally acceptable according to the licenses of a particular profession. This definition should be described in the licensing regulation. The education process of the profession helps determine the scope of practice. The skills learned and training received is directly related to the scope of practice of the occupation.

81. A: When the client is lying in the supine position, a bolster should be used behind the knees to reduce tension in the low back and back of the legs.

82. D: Afferent neurons carry signals of touch, cold, heat, sight, hearing, taste, or pain from the sensory organs of the body to the brain, where they are interpreted.

83. D: When the client is rolling over, the practitioner can secure the draping by leaning into the table and holding the drape in place while grasping the drape at the level of the client's shoulders and hips. The drape can then be lifted to allow the client to reposition and remain secure.

84. D: A tendon is not inert tissue. It is contractile tissue. Muscle and tendon are contractile tissues. Inert tissues are not contractile

85. A: A mission statement expresses the values of the business. It is a short, general statement that explains the main focus of the business. It can be used in advertising and promotional materials and should be carefully considered. This is the statement that reflects the business's public image.

86. A: The practitioner should always request a doctor's recommendation before treating a client with cancer. It is important to work closely with the client's medical team and have a full understanding of the illness and current treatment plan. The practitioner should remain in contact with the physician to be aware of any change in condition and treatment recommendations.

87. C: There are three criteria the Internal Revenue Service uses to define a relationship as an independent contractor as opposed to an employee. One criterion is that the independent contractor must be able to set the work hours and the manner in which the work is done. An independent contractor must also have financial control by paying either a flat fee or rent or receiving commission based on work completed. The independent contractor does not receive vacation pay, sick days, or benefits. The independent contractor relationship is usually defined in a contract signed by both parties.

88. A: Increasing blood flow to the tumor site is not a benefit of massage to a person with cancer. Massage will boost the healing process, reduce edema, and improve lymph flow. It will also relieve stress, promote relaxation, help with insomnia, and reduce anxiety as well as many other benefits.

89. B: A corporation is a legal business entity that is separate from any individual or individuals. A charter must be obtained in the state the corporation is operating in. The corporation is managed by a board of directors and has stockholders who share in the profits but are not legally responsible for the actions of the corporation. The corporation is taxed separately from any shareholders.

90. A: Inert tissue is any tissue that is not contractile. This would include bone, ligament, bursa, nerve, blood vessels, and cartilage. Tendon and muscle are contractile tissues.

91. B: Food passes through the esophagus and in to the stomach. Gastric juices containing hydrochloric acid and digestive enzymes mix with the food and mucus to create chyme. This mixture then passes into the small intestine.

92. D: Neuromuscular therapy addresses trigger points and their relationship to local and referred pain by using anatomic knowledge and palpatory skills to assess the condition of the tissue and treat neuromuscular lesions. These neuromuscular lesions are often sensitive to pressure and are affiliated with trigger points. The treatment normalizes the tissue and breaks the cycle of pain and dysfunction.

93. A: The anterior fibers of the deltoid muscle originate on the lateral one-third of the clavicle and insert into the deltoid tuberosity of the humerus.

94. C: The lumbar plexus is formed by the first four of the five lumbar nerves. These nerves supply the skin, the abdominal organs, and the hip, knee, leg, and thigh. The femoral and obturator nerves are part of the lumbar plexus.

95. D: A dual relationship is a relationship that consists of both a therapeutic relationship between the practitioner and client as well as a secondary relationship that is outside of the normal therapeutic environment.

96. C: The antagonist is the muscle that opposes the prime mover. The antagonist must perform the opposite action of the prime mover to allow the movement to happen. For example, when lifting a cup, the biceps will contract to perform the movement, whereas the triceps lengthen and extend in the opposing direction to allow the movement.

97. A: The three normal end feels are hard, soft, and springy. A hard end feel is one that is abrupt and painless and feels like bone on bone. A soft end feel is one where soft tissue prevents any further movement. A springy end feel is created by the stretch of fibrous tissue at the end of the range of motion.

98. D: Tylenol is classified as a non-opioid analgesic. It is sold over the counter and is used to relieve mild to moderate pain, fever, and some inflammatory conditions like arthritis. Non-opioid analgesics are not considered habit-forming and do not cause withdrawal symptoms.

99. C: Transference happens in a therapeutic relationship when a client personalizes the relationship and begins to unconsciously project characteristics of someone from a previous relationship onto the practitioner. The client may have misperceptions regarding the intent of the relationship. Signs of transference include the giving of gifts, asking personal questions, and attempts to befriend the practitioner.

100. A: If a client has already been referred by a physician and no injury was found, the practitioner should reassess the client and evaluate whether the treatment plan is effective. If the practitioner creates a new treatment plan that does not show results after a few sessions, then the client should return to the original physician for follow-up care.

Photo Credits

Licensed Under CC BY 4.0 (creativecommons.org/licenses/by/4.0/)

Muscles: "The Three Connective Tissue Layers" by Openstax Anatomy & Physiology Chapter 10.2 (https://cnx.org/contents/FPtK1zmh@8.25:bfiqsxdB@3/Skeletal-Muscle)
Human skeleton: "Human skeleton front en" by Mariana Ruiz Villarreal (https://commons.wikimedia.org/wiki/File:Human_skeleton_front_en.svg)
Cardiovascular System: "Circulatory System en edited" by Mariana Ruiz Villarreal (https://commons.wikimedia.org/wiki/File:Circulatory_System_en_edited.svg)
Muscular System: "Overview of Muscular System" by Openstax Anatomy & Physiology Chapter 11.2 (https://cnx.org/contents/FPtK1zmh@8.25:FL6Dj0EF@3/Naming-Skeletal-Muscles)

Licensed Under CC BY-SA 3.0 (creativecommons.org/licenses/by-sa/3.0/deed.en)

Planes of Movement: "Human anatomy planes" by YassineMrabet (https://commons.wikimedia.org/wiki/File:Human_anatomy_planes.svg)

Secret Key #1 - Time is Your Greatest Enemy

Pace Yourself

Wear a watch. At the beginning of the test, check the time (or start a chronometer on your watch to count the minutes), and check the time after every few questions to make sure you are "on schedule."

If you are forced to speed up, do it efficiently. Usually one or more answer choices can be eliminated without too much difficulty. Above all, don't panic. Don't speed up and just begin guessing at random choices. By pacing yourself, and continually monitoring your progress against your watch, you will always know exactly how far ahead or behind you are with your available time. If you find that you are one minute behind on the test, don't skip one question without spending any time on it, just to catch back up. Take 15 fewer seconds on the next four questions, and after four questions you'll have caught back up. Once you catch back up, you can continue working each problem at your normal pace.

Furthermore, don't dwell on the problems that you were rushed on. If a problem was taking up too much time and you made a hurried guess, it must be difficult. The difficult questions are the ones you are most likely to miss anyway, so it isn't a big loss. It is better to end with more time than you need than to run out of time.

Lastly, sometimes it is beneficial to slow down if you are constantly getting ahead of time. You are always more likely to catch a careless mistake by working more slowly than quickly, and among very high-scoring test takers (those who are likely to have lots of time left over), careless errors affect the score more than mastery of material.

Secret Key #2 - Guessing is not Guesswork

You probably know that guessing is a good idea. Unlike other standardized tests, there is no penalty for getting a wrong answer. Even if you have no idea about a question, you still have a 20-25% chance of getting it right.

Most test takers do not understand the impact that proper guessing can have on their score. Unless you score extremely high, guessing will significantly contribute to your final score.

Monkeys Take the Test

What most test takers don't realize is that to insure that 20-25% chance, you have to guess randomly. If you put 20 monkeys in a room to take this test, assuming they answered once per question and behaved themselves, on average they would get 20-25% of the questions correct. Put 20 test takers in the room, and the average will be much lower among guessed questions. Why?
1. The test writers intentionally write deceptive answer choices that "look" right. A test taker has no idea about a question, so he picks the "best looking" answer, which is often wrong. The monkey has no idea what looks good and what doesn't, so it will consistently be right about 20-25% of the time.
2. Test takers will eliminate answer choices from the guessing pool based on a hunch or intuition. Simple but correct answers often get excluded, leaving a 0% chance of being correct. The monkey has no clue, and often gets lucky with the best choice.

This is why the process of elimination endorsed by most test courses is flawed and detrimental to your performance. Test takers don't guess; they make an ignorant stab in the dark that is usually worse than random.

$5 Challenge

Let me introduce one of the most valuable ideas of this course—the $5 challenge:

You only mark your "best guess" if you are willing to bet $5 on it.
You only eliminate choices from guessing if you are willing to bet $5 on it.

Why $5? Five dollars is an amount of money that is small yet not insignificant, and can really add up fast (20 questions could cost you $100). Likewise, each answer choice on one question of the test will have a small impact on your overall score, but it can really add up to a lot of points in the end.

The process of elimination IS valuable. The following shows your chance of guessing it right:

If you eliminate wrong answer choices until only this many remain:	Chance of getting it correct:
1	100%
2	50%
3	33%

However, if you accidentally eliminate the right answer or go on a hunch for an incorrect answer, your chances drop dramatically—to 0%. By guessing among all the answer choices, you are GUARANTEED to have a shot at the right answer.

That's why the $5 test is so valuable. If you give up the advantage and safety of a pure guess, it had better be worth the risk.

What we still haven't covered is how to be sure that whatever guess you make is truly random. Here's the easiest way:

Always pick the first answer choice among those remaining.

Such a technique means that you have decided, **before you see a single test question**, exactly how you are going to guess, and since the order of choices tells you nothing about which one is correct, this guessing technique is perfectly random.

This section is not meant to scare you away from making educated guesses or eliminating choices; you just need to define when a choice is worth eliminating. The $5 test, along with a pre-defined random guessing strategy, is the best way to make sure you reap all of the benefits of guessing.

Secret Key #3 - Practice Smarter, Not Harder

Many test takers delay the test preparation process because they dread the awful amounts of practice time they think necessary to succeed on the test. We have refined an effective method that will take you only a fraction of the time.

There are a number of "obstacles" in the path to success. Among these are answering questions, finishing in time, and mastering test-taking strategies. All must be executed on the day of the test at peak performance, or your score will suffer. The test is a mental marathon that has a large impact on your future.

Just like a marathon runner, it is important to work your way up to the full challenge. So first you just worry about questions, and then time, and finally strategy:

Success Strategy

1. Find a good source for practice tests.
2. If you are willing to make a larger time investment, consider using more than one study guide. Often the different approaches of multiple authors will help you "get" difficult concepts.
3. Take a practice test with no time constraints, with all study helps, "open book." Take your time with questions and focus on applying strategies.
4. Take a practice test with time constraints, with all guides, "open book."
5. Take a final practice test without open material and with time limits.

If you have time to take more practice tests, just repeat step 5. By gradually exposing yourself to the full rigors of the test environment, you will condition your mind to the stress of test day and maximize your success.

Secret Key #4 - Prepare, Don't Procrastinate

Let me state an obvious fact: if you take the test three times, you will probably get three different scores. This is due to the way you feel on test day, the level of preparedness you have, and the version of the test you see. Despite the test writers' claims to the contrary, some versions of the test WILL be easier for you than others.

Since your future depends so much on your score, you should maximize your chances of success. In order to maximize the likelihood of success, you've got to prepare in advance. This means taking practice tests and spending time learning the information and test taking strategies you will need to succeed.

Never go take the actual test as a "practice" test, expecting that you can just take it again if you need to. Take all the practice tests you can on your own, but when you go to take the official test, be prepared, be focused, and do your best the first time!

Secret Key #5 - Test Yourself

Everyone knows that time is money. There is no need to spend too much of your time or too little of your time preparing for the test. You should only spend as much of your precious time preparing as is necessary for you to get the score you need.

Once you have taken a practice test under real conditions of time constraints, then you will know if you are ready for the test or not.

If you have scored extremely high the first time that you take the practice test, then there is not much point in spending countless hours studying. You are already there.

Benchmark your abilities by retaking practice tests and seeing how much you have improved. Once you consistently score high enough to guarantee success, then you are ready.

If you have scored well below where you need, then knuckle down and begin studying in earnest. Check your improvement regularly through the use of practice tests under real conditions. Above all, don't worry, panic, or give up. The key is perseverance!

Then, when you go to take the test, remain confident and remember how well you did on the practice tests. If you can score high enough on a practice test, then you can do the same on the real thing.

General Strategies

The most important thing you can do is to ignore your fears and jump into the test immediately. Do not be overwhelmed by any strange-sounding terms. You have to jump into the test like jumping into a pool—all at once is the easiest way.

Make Predictions

As you read and understand the question, try to guess what the answer will be. Remember that several of the answer choices are wrong, and once you begin reading them, your mind will immediately become cluttered with answer choices designed to throw you off. Your mind is typically the most focused immediately after you have read the question and digested its contents. If you can, try to predict what the correct answer will be. You may be surprised at what you can predict.

Quickly scan the choices and see if your prediction is in the listed answer choices. If it is, then you can be quite confident that you have the right answer. It still won't hurt to check the other answer choices, but most of the time, you've got it!

Answer the Question

It may seem obvious to only pick answer choices that answer the question, but the test writers can create some excellent answer choices that are wrong. Don't pick an answer just because it sounds right, or you believe it to be true. It MUST answer the question. Once you've made your selection, always go back and check it against the question and make sure that you didn't misread the question and that the answer choice does answer the question posed.

Benchmark

After you read the first answer choice, decide if you think it sounds correct or not. If it doesn't, move on to the next answer choice. If it does, mentally mark that answer choice. This doesn't mean that you've definitely selected it as your answer choice, it just means that it's the best you've seen thus far. Go ahead and read the next choice. If the next choice is worse than the one you've already selected, keep going to the next answer choice. If the next choice is better than the choice you've already selected, mentally mark the new answer choice as your best guess.

The first answer choice that you select becomes your standard. Every other answer choice must be benchmarked against that standard. That choice is correct until proven otherwise by another answer choice beating it out. Once you've decided that no other answer choice seems as good, do one final check to ensure that your answer choice answers the question posed.

Valid Information

Don't discount any of the information provided in the question. Every piece of information may be necessary to determine the correct answer. None of the information in the question is there to throw you off (while the answer choices will certainly have information to throw you off). If two seemingly unrelated topics are discussed, don't ignore either. You can be confident there is a relationship, or it wouldn't be included in the question, and you are probably going to have to determine what is that relationship to find the answer.

Avoid "Fact Traps"

Don't get distracted by a choice that is factually true. Your search is for the answer that answers the question. Stay focused and don't fall for an answer that is true but irrelevant. Always go back to the question and make sure you're choosing an answer that actually answers the question and is not just a true statement. An answer can be factually correct, but it MUST answer the question asked. Additionally, two answers can both be seemingly correct, so be sure to read all of the answer choices, and make sure that you get the one that BEST answers the question.

Milk the Question

Some of the questions may throw you completely off. They might deal with a subject you have not been exposed to, or one that you haven't reviewed in years. While your lack of knowledge about the subject will be a hindrance, the question itself can give you many clues that will help you find the correct answer. Read the question carefully and look for clues. Watch particularly for adjectives and nouns describing difficult terms or words that you don't recognize. Regardless of whether you completely understand a word or not, replacing it with a synonym, either provided or one you more familiar with, may help you to understand what the questions are asking. Rather than wracking your mind about specific detailed information concerning a difficult term or word, try to use mental substitutes that are easier to understand.

The Trap of Familiarity

Don't just choose a word because you recognize it. On difficult questions, you may not recognize a number of words in the answer choices. The test writers don't put "make-believe" words on the test, so don't think that just because you only recognize all the words in one answer choice that that answer choice must be correct. If you only recognize words in one answer choice, then focus on that one. Is it correct? Try your best to determine if it is correct. If it is, that's great. If not, eliminate it. Each word and answer choice you eliminate increases your chances of getting the question correct, even if you then have to guess among the unfamiliar choices.

Eliminate Answers

Eliminate choices as soon as you realize they are wrong. But be careful! Make sure you consider all of the possible answer choices. Just because one appears right, doesn't mean that the next one won't be even better! The test writers will usually put more than one good answer choice for every question, so read all of them. Don't worry if you are stuck between two that seem right. By getting down to just two remaining possible choices, your odds are now 50/50. Rather than wasting too much time, play the odds. You are guessing, but guessing wisely because you've been able to knock out some of the answer choices that you know are wrong. If you are eliminating choices and realize that the last answer choice you are left with is also obviously wrong, don't panic. Start over and consider each choice again. There may easily be something that you missed the first time and will realize on the second pass.

Tough Questions

If you are stumped on a problem or it appears too hard or too difficult, don't waste time. Move on! Remember though, if you can quickly check for obviously incorrect answer choices, your chances of guessing correctly are greatly improved. Before you completely give up, at least try to knock out a couple of possible answers. Eliminate what you can and then guess at the remaining answer choices before moving on.

Brainstorm

If you get stuck on a difficult question, spend a few seconds quickly brainstorming. Run through the complete list of possible answer choices. Look at each choice and ask yourself, "Could this answer the question satisfactorily?" Go through each answer choice and consider it independently of the others. By systematically going through all possibilities, you may find something that you would otherwise overlook. Remember though that when you get stuck, it's important to try to keep moving.

Read Carefully

Understand the problem. Read the question and answer choices carefully. Don't miss the question because you misread the terms. You have plenty of time to read each question thoroughly and make sure you understand what is being asked. Yet a happy medium must be attained, so don't waste too much time. You must read carefully, but efficiently.

Face Value

When in doubt, use common sense. Always accept the situation in the problem at face value. Don't read too much into it. These problems will not require you to make huge leaps of logic. The test writers aren't trying to throw you off with a cheap trick. If you have to go beyond creativity and make a leap of logic in order to have an answer choice answer the question, then you should look at the other answer choices. Don't overcomplicate the problem by creating theoretical relationships or explanations that will warp time or space. These are normal problems rooted in reality. It's just that the applicable relationship or explanation may not be readily apparent and you have to figure things out. Use your common sense to interpret anything that isn't clear.

Prefixes

If you're having trouble with a word in the question or answer choices, try dissecting it. Take advantage of every clue that the word might include. Prefixes and suffixes can be a huge help. Usually they allow you to determine a basic meaning. Pre- means before, post- means after, pro - is positive, de- is negative. From these prefixes and suffixes, you can get an idea of the general meaning of the word and try to put it into context. Beware though of any traps. Just because con- is the opposite of pro-, doesn't necessarily mean congress is the opposite of progress!

Hedge Phrases

Watch out for critical hedge phrases, led off with words such as "likely," "may," "can," "sometimes," "often," "almost," "mostly," "usually," "generally," "rarely," and "sometimes." Question writers insert these hedge phrases to cover every possibility. Often an answer choice will be wrong simply because it leaves no room for exception. Unless the situation calls for them, avoid answer choices that have definitive words like "exactly," and "always."

Switchback Words

Stay alert for "switchbacks." These are the words and phrases frequently used to alert you to shifts in thought. The most common switchback word is "but." Others include "although," "however," "nevertheless," "on the other hand," "even though," "while," "in spite of," "despite," and "regardless of."

New Information

Correct answer choices will rarely have completely new information included. Answer choices typically are straightforward reflections of the material asked about and will directly relate to the question. If a new piece of information is included in an answer choice that doesn't even seem to relate to the topic being asked about, then that answer choice is likely incorrect. All of the information needed to answer the question is usually provided for you in the question. You should not have to make guesses that are unsupported or choose answer choices that require unknown information that cannot be reasoned from what is given.

Time Management

On technical questions, don't get lost on the technical terms. Don't spend too much time on any one question. If you don't know what a term means, then odds are you aren't going to get much further since you don't have a dictionary. You should be able to immediately recognize whether or not you know a term. If you don't, work with the other clues that you have—the other answer choices and terms provided—but don't waste too much time trying to figure out a difficult term that you don't know.

Contextual Clues

Look for contextual clues. An answer can be right but not the correct answer. The contextual clues will help you find the answer that is most right and is correct. Understand the context in which a phrase or statement is made. This will help you make important distinctions.

Don't Panic

Panicking will not answer any questions for you; therefore, it isn't helpful. When you first see the question, if your mind goes blank, take a deep breath. Force yourself to mechanically go through the steps of solving the problem using the strategies you've learned.

Pace Yourself

Don't get clock fever. It's easy to be overwhelmed when you're looking at a page full of questions, your mind is full of random thoughts and feeling confused, and the clock is ticking down faster than you would like. Calm down and maintain the pace that you have set for yourself. As long as you are on track by monitoring your pace, you are guaranteed to have enough time for yourself. When you get to the last few minutes of the test, it may seem like you won't have enough time left, but if you only have as many questions as you should have left at that point, then you're right on track!

Answer Selection

The best way to pick an answer choice is to eliminate all of those that are wrong, until only one is left and confirm that is the correct answer. Sometimes though, an answer choice may immediately look right. Be careful! Take a second to make sure that the other choices are not equally obvious. Don't make a hasty mistake. There are only two times that you should stop before checking other answers. First is when you are positive that the answer choice you have selected is correct. Second is when time is almost out and you have to make a quick guess!

Check Your Work

Since you will probably not know every term listed and the answer to every question, it is important that you get credit for the ones that you do know. Don't miss any questions through careless mistakes. If at all possible, try to take a second to look back over your answer selection and make sure you've selected the correct answer choice and haven't made a costly careless mistake (such as marking an answer choice that you didn't mean to mark). The time it takes for this quick double check should more than pay for itself in caught mistakes.

Beware of Directly Quoted Answers

Sometimes an answer choice will repeat word for word a portion of the question or reference section. However, beware of such exact duplication. It may be a trap! More than likely, the correct choice will paraphrase or summarize a point, rather than being exactly the same wording.

Slang

Scientific sounding answers are better than slang ones. An answer choice that begins "To compare the outcomes..." is much more likely to be correct than one that begins "Because some people insisted..."

Extreme Statements

Avoid wild answers that throw out highly controversial ideas that are proclaimed as established fact. An answer choice that states the "process should used in certain situations, if..." is much more likely to be correct than one that states the "process should be discontinued completely." The first is a calm rational statement and doesn't even make a definitive, uncompromising stance, using a hedge word "if" to provide wiggle room, whereas the second choice is a radical idea and far more extreme.

Answer Choice Families

When you have two or more answer choices that are direct opposites or parallels, one of them is usually the correct answer. For instance, if one answer choice states "x increases" and another answer choice states "x decreases" or "y increases," then those two or three answer choices are very similar in construction and fall into the same family of answer choices. A family of answer choices consists of two or three answer choices, very similar in construction, but often with directly opposite meanings. Usually the correct answer choice will be in that family of answer choices. The "odd man out" or answer choice that doesn't seem to fit the parallel construction of the other answer choices is more likely to be incorrect.

Special Report: How to Overcome Test Anxiety

The very nature of tests caters to some level of anxiety, nervousness, or tension, just as we feel for any important event that occurs in our lives. A little bit of anxiety or nervousness can be a good thing. It helps us with motivation, and makes achievement just that much sweeter. However, too much anxiety can be a problem, especially if it hinders our ability to function and perform.

"Test anxiety," is the term that refers to the emotional reactions that some test-takers experience when faced with a test or exam. Having a fear of testing and exams is based upon a rational fear, since the test-taker's performance can shape the course of an academic career. Nevertheless, experiencing excessive fear of examinations will only interfere with the test-taker's ability to perform and chance to be successful.

There are a large variety of causes that can contribute to the development and sensation of test anxiety. These include, but are not limited to, lack of preparation and worrying about issues surrounding the test.

Lack of Preparation

Lack of preparation can be identified by the following behaviors or situations:
- Not scheduling enough time to study, and therefore cramming the night before the test or exam
- Managing time poorly, to create the sensation that there is not enough time to do everything
- Failing to organize the text information in advance, so that the study material consists of the entire text and not simply the pertinent information
- Poor overall studying habits

Worrying, on the other hand, can be related to both the test taker, or many other factors around him/her that will be affected by the results of the test. These include worrying about:
- Previous performances on similar exams, or exams in general
- How friends and other students are achieving
- The negative consequences that will result from a poor grade or failure

There are three primary elements to test anxiety. Physical components, which involve the same typical bodily reactions as those to acute anxiety (to be discussed below). Emotional factors have to do with fear or panic. Mental or cognitive issues concerning attention spans and memory abilities.

Physical Signals

There are many different symptoms of test anxiety, and these are not limited to mental and emotional strain. Frequently there are a range of physical signals that will let a test taker know that he/she is suffering from test anxiety. These bodily changes can include the following:

- Perspiring
- Sweaty palms
- Wet, trembling hands
- Nausea
- Dry mouth
- A knot in the stomach
- Headache
- Faintness
- Muscle tension
- Aching shoulders, back and neck
- Rapid heart beat
- Feeling too hot/cold

To recognize the sensation of test anxiety, a test-taker should monitor him/herself for the following sensations:

The physical distress symptoms as listed above
Emotional sensitivity, expressing emotional feelings such as the need to cry or laugh too much, or a sensation of anger or helplessness
A decreased ability to think, causing the test-taker to blank out or have racing thoughts that are hard to organize or control.

Though most students will feel some level of anxiety when faced with a test or exam, the majority can cope with that anxiety and maintain it at a manageable level. However, those who cannot are faced with a very real and very serious condition, which can and should be controlled for the immeasurable benefit of this sufferer.

Naturally, these sensations lead to negative results for the testing experience. The most common effects of test anxiety have to do with nervousness and mental blocking.

Nervousness

Nervousness can appear in several different levels:
- The test-taker's difficulty, or even inability to read and understand the questions on the test
- The difficulty or inability to organize thoughts to a coherent form
- The difficulty or inability to recall key words and concepts relating to the testing questions (especially essays)
- The receipt of poor grades on a test, though the test material was well known by the test taker

Conversely, a person may also experience mental blocking, which involves:
- Blanking out on test questions
- Only remembering the correct answers to the questions when the test has already finished.

Fortunately for test anxiety sufferers, beating these feelings, to a large degree, has to do with proper preparation. When a test taker has a feeling of preparedness, then anxiety will be dramatically lessened.

The first step to resolving anxiety issues is to distinguish which of the two types of anxiety are being suffered. If the anxiety is a direct result of a lack of preparation, this should be considered a normal reaction, and the anxiety level (as opposed to the test results) shouldn't be anything to worry about. However, if, when adequately prepared, the test-taker still panics, blanks out, or seems to overreact, this is not a fully rational reaction. While this can be considered normal too, there are many ways to combat and overcome these effects.

Remember that anxiety cannot be entirely eliminated, however, there are ways to minimize it, to make the anxiety easier to manage. Preparation is one of the best ways to minimize test anxiety. Therefore the following techniques are wise in order to best fight off any anxiety that may want to build.

To begin with, try to avoid cramming before a test, whenever it is possible. By trying to memorize an entire term's worth of information in one day, you'll be shocking your system, and not giving yourself a very good chance to absorb the information. This is an easy path to anxiety, so for those who suffer from test anxiety, cramming should not even be considered an option.

Instead of cramming, work throughout the semester to combine all of the material which is presented throughout the semester, and work on it gradually as the course goes by, making sure to master the main concepts first, leaving minor details for a week or so before the test.

To study for the upcoming exam, be sure to pose questions that may be on the examination, to gauge the ability to answer them by integrating the ideas from your texts, notes and lectures, as well as any supplementary readings.

If it is truly impossible to cover all of the information that was covered in that particular term, concentrate on the most important portions, that can be covered very well. Learn these concepts as best as possible, so that when the test comes, a goal can be made to use these concepts as presentations of your knowledge.

In addition to study habits, changes in attitude are critical to beating a struggle with test anxiety. In fact, an improvement of the perspective over the entire test-taking experience can actually help a test taker to enjoy studying and therefore improve the overall experience. Be certain not to overemphasize the significance of the grade - know that the result of the test is neither a reflection of self-worth, nor is it a measure of intelligence; one grade will not predict a person's future success.

To improve an overall testing outlook, the following steps should be tried:
- Keeping in mind that the most reasonable expectation for taking a test is to expect to try to demonstrate as much of what you know as you possibly can.
- Reminding ourselves that a test is only one test; this is not the only one, and there will be others.

- The thought of thinking of oneself in an irrational, all-or-nothing term should be avoided at all costs.
- A reward should be designated for after the test, so there's something to look forward to. Whether it be going to a movie, going out to eat, or simply visiting friends, schedule it in advance, and do it no matter what result is expected on the exam.

Test-takers should also keep in mind that the basics are some of the most important things, even beyond anti-anxiety techniques and studying. Never neglect the basic social, emotional and biological needs, in order to try to absorb information. In order to best achieve, these three factors must be held as just as important as the studying itself.

Study Steps

Remember the following important steps for studying:
- Maintain healthy nutrition and exercise habits. Continue both your recreational activities and social pass times. These both contribute to your physical and emotional wellbeing.
- Be certain to get a good amount of sleep, especially the night before the test, because when you're overtired you are not able to perform to the best of your best ability.
- Keep the studying pace to a moderate level by taking breaks when they are needed, and varying the work whenever possible, to keep the mind fresh instead of getting bored.
- When enough studying has been done that all the material that can be learned has been learned, and the test taker is prepared for the test, stop studying and do something relaxing such as listening to music, watching a movie, or taking a warm bubble bath.

There are also many other techniques to minimize the uneasiness or apprehension that is experienced along with test anxiety before, during, or even after the examination. In fact, there are a great deal of things that can be done to stop anxiety from interfering with lifestyle and performance. Again, remember that anxiety will not be eliminated entirely, and it shouldn't be. Otherwise that "up" feeling for exams would not exist, and most of us depend on that sensation to perform better than usual. However, this anxiety has to be at a level that is manageable.

Of course, as we have just discussed, being prepared for the exam is half the battle right away. Attending all classes, finding out what knowledge will be expected on the exam, and knowing the exam schedules are easy steps to lowering anxiety. Keeping up with work will remove the need to cram, and efficient study habits will eliminate wasted time. Studying should be done in an ideal location for concentration, so that it is simple to become interested in the material and give it complete attention. A method such as SQ3R (Survey, Question, Read, Recite, Review) is a wonderful key to follow to make sure that the study habits are as effective as possible, especially in the case of learning from a textbook. Flashcards are great techniques for memorization. Learning to take good notes will mean that notes will be full of useful information, so that less sifting will need to be done to seek out what is pertinent for studying. Reviewing notes after class and then again on occasion will keep the information fresh in the mind. From notes that have been taken summary sheets and outlines can be made for simpler reviewing.

A study group can also be a very motivational and helpful place to study, as there will be a sharing of ideas, all of the minds can work together, to make sure that everyone understands, and the studying will be made more interesting because it will be a social occasion.

Basically, though, as long as the test-taker remains organized and self confident, with efficient study habits, less time will need to be spent studying, and higher grades will be achieved.

To become self confident, there are many useful steps. The first of these is "self talk." It has been shown through extensive research, that self-talk for students who suffer from test anxiety, should be well monitored, in order to make sure that it contributes to self confidence as opposed to sinking the student. Frequently the self talk of test-anxious students is negative or self-defeating, thinking that everyone else is smarter and faster, that they always mess up, and that if they don't do well, they'll fail the entire course. It is important to decreasing anxiety that awareness is made of self talk. Try writing any negative self thoughts and then disputing them with a positive statement instead. Begin self-encouragement as though it was a friend speaking. Repeat positive statements to help reprogram the mind to believing in successes instead of failures.

Helpful Techniques

Other extremely helpful techniques include:
- Self-visualization of doing well and reaching goals
- While aiming for an "A" level of understanding, don't try to "overprotect" by setting your expectations lower. This will only convince the mind to stop studying in order to meet the lower expectations.
- Don't make comparisons with the results or habits of other students. These are individual factors, and different things work for different people, causing different results.
- Strive to become an expert in learning what works well, and what can be done in order to improve. Consider collecting this data in a journal.
- Create rewards for after studying instead of doing things before studying that will only turn into avoidance behaviors.
- Make a practice of relaxing - by using methods such as progressive relaxation, self-hypnosis, guided imagery, etc - in order to make relaxation an automatic sensation.
- Work on creating a state of relaxed concentration so that concentrating will take on the focus of the mind, so that none will be wasted on worrying.
- Take good care of the physical self by eating well and getting enough sleep.
- Plan in time for exercise and stick to this plan.

Beyond these techniques, there are other methods to be used before, during and after the test that will help the test-taker perform well in addition to overcoming anxiety.

Before the exam comes the academic preparation. This involves establishing a study schedule and beginning at least one week before the actual date of the test. By doing this, the anxiety of not having enough time to study for the test will be automatically eliminated. Moreover, this will make the studying a much more effective experience, ensuring that the learning will be an easier process. This relieves much undue pressure on the test-taker.

Summary sheets, note cards, and flash cards with the main concepts and examples of these main concepts should be prepared in advance of the actual studying time. A topic should never be eliminated from this process. By omitting a topic because it isn't expected to be on the test is only setting up the test-taker for anxiety should it actually appear on the exam. Utilize the course syllabus for laying out the topics that should be studied. Carefully go over the notes that were made in class, paying special attention to any of the issues that the professor took special care to emphasize while lecturing in class. In the textbooks, use the chapter review, or if possible, the chapter tests, to begin your review.

It may even be possible to ask the instructor what information will be covered on the exam, or what the format of the exam will be (for example, multiple choice, essay, free form, true-false). Additionally, see if it is possible to find out how many questions will be on the test. If a review sheet or sample test has been offered by the professor, make good use of it, above anything else, for the preparation for the test. Another great resource for getting to know the examination is reviewing tests from previous semesters. Use these tests to review, and aim to achieve a 100% score on each of the possible topics. With a few exceptions, the goal that you set for yourself is the highest one that you will reach.

Take all of the questions that were assigned as homework, and rework them to any other possible course material. The more problems reworked, the more skill and confidence will form as a result. When forming the solution to a problem, write out each of the steps. Don't simply do head work. By doing as many steps on paper as possible, much clarification and therefore confidence will be formed. Do this with as many homework problems as possible, before checking the answers. By checking the answer after each problem, a reinforcement will exist, that will not be on the exam. Study situations should be as exam-like as possible, to prime the test-taker's system for the experience. By waiting to check the answers at the end, a psychological advantage will be formed, to decrease the stress factor.

Another fantastic reason for not cramming is the avoidance of confusion in concepts, especially when it comes to mathematics. 8-10 hours of study will become one hundred percent more effective if it is spread out over a week or at least several days, instead of doing it all in one sitting. Recognize that the human brain requires time in order to assimilate new material, so frequent breaks and a span of study time over several days will be much more beneficial.

Additionally, don't study right up until the point of the exam. Studying should stop a minimum of one hour before the exam begins. This allows the brain to rest and put things in their proper order. This will also provide the time to become as relaxed as possible when going into the examination room. The test-taker will also have time to eat well and eat sensibly. Know that the brain needs food as much as the rest of the body. With enough food and enough sleep, as well as a relaxed attitude, the body and the mind are primed for success.

Avoid any anxious classmates who are talking about the exam. These students only spread anxiety, and are not worth sharing the anxious sentimentalities.

Before the test also involves creating a positive attitude, so mental preparation should also be a point of concentration. There are many keys to creating a positive attitude. Should fears become rushing in, make a visualization of taking the exam, doing well, and seeing an A written on the paper. Write out a list of affirmations that will bring a feeling of confidence, such as "I am doing well in my English class," "I studied well and know my material," "I enjoy this class." Even if the affirmations aren't believed at first, it sends a positive message to the subconscious which will result in an alteration of the overall belief system, which is the system that creates reality.

If a sensation of panic begins, work with the fear and imagine the very worst! Work through the entire scenario of not passing the test, failing the entire course, and dropping out of school, followed by not getting a job, and pushing a shopping cart through the dark alley where you'll live. This will place things into perspective! Then, practice deep breathing and create a visualization of the opposite situation - achieving an "A" on the exam, passing the entire course, receiving the degree at a graduation ceremony.

On the day of the test, there are many things to be done to ensure the best results, as well as the most calm outlook. The following stages are suggested in order to maximize test-taking potential:

1. Begin the examination day with a moderate breakfast, and avoid any coffee or beverages with caffeine if the test taker is prone to jitters. Even people who are used to managing caffeine can feel jittery or light-headed when it is taken on a test day.
2. Attempt to do something that is relaxing before the examination begins. As last minute cramming clouds the mastering of overall concepts, it is better to use this time to create a calming outlook.
3. Be certain to arrive at the test location well in advance, in order to provide time to select a location that is away from doors, windows and other distractions, as well as giving enough time to relax before the test begins.
4. Keep away from anxiety generating classmates who will upset the sensation of stability and relaxation that is being attempted before the exam.
5. Should the waiting period before the exam begins cause anxiety, create a self-distraction by reading a light magazine or something else that is relaxing and simple.

During the exam itself, read the entire exam from beginning to end, and find out how much time should be allotted to each individual problem. Once writing the exam, should more time be taken for a problem, it should be abandoned, in order to begin another problem. If there is time at the end, the unfinished problem can always be returned to and completed.

Read the instructions very carefully - twice - so that unpleasant surprises won't follow during or after the exam has ended.

When writing the exam, pretend that the situation is actually simply the completion of homework within a library, or at home. This will assist in forming a relaxed atmosphere, and will allow the brain extra focus for the complex thinking function.

Begin the exam with all of the questions with which the most confidence is felt. This will build the confidence level regarding the entire exam and will begin a quality momentum. This will also create encouragement for trying the problems where uncertainty resides.

Going with the "gut instinct" is always the way to go when solving a problem. Second guessing should be avoided at all costs. Have confidence in the ability to do well.

For essay questions, create an outline in advance that will keep the mind organized and make certain that all of the points are remembered. For multiple choice, read every answer, even if the correct one has been spotted - a better one may exist.

Continue at a pace that is reasonable and not rushed, in order to be able to work carefully. Provide enough time to go over the answers at the end, to check for small errors that can be corrected.

Should a feeling of panic begin, breathe deeply, and think of the feeling of the body releasing sand through its pores. Visualize a calm, peaceful place, and include all of the sights, sounds and sensations of this image. Continue the deep breathing, and take a few minutes to continue this with closed eyes. When all is well again, return to the test.

If a "blanking" occurs for a certain question, skip it and move on to the next question. There will be time to return to the other question later. Get everything done that can be done, first, to guarantee all the grades that can be compiled, and to build all of the confidence possible. Then return to the weaker questions to build the marks from there.

Remember, one's own reality can be created, so as long as the belief is there, success will follow. And remember: anxiety can happen later, right now, there's an exam to be written!

After the examination is complete, whether there is a feeling for a good grade or a bad grade, don't dwell on the exam, and be certain to follow through on the reward that was promised...and enjoy it! Don't dwell on any mistakes that have been made, as there is nothing that can be done at this point anyway.

Additionally, don't begin to study for the next test right away. Do something relaxing for a while, and let the mind relax and prepare itself to begin absorbing information again.

From the results of the exam - both the grade and the entire experience, be certain to learn from what has gone on. Perfect studying habits and work some more on confidence in order to make the next examination experience even better than the last one.

Learn to avoid places where openings occurred for laziness, procrastination and day dreaming.

Use the time between this exam and the next one to better learn to relax, even learning to relax on cue, so that any anxiety can be controlled during the next exam. Learn how to relax the body. Slouch in your chair if that helps. Tighten and then relax all of the different muscle groups, one group at a time, beginning with the feet and then working all the way up to the neck and face. This will ultimately relax the muscles more than they were to begin with. Learn how to breathe deeply and comfortably, and focus on this breathing going in and out as a relaxing thought. With every exhale, repeat the word "relax."

As common as test anxiety is, it is very possible to overcome it. Make yourself one of the test-takers who overcome this frustrating hindrance.

Additional Bonus Material

Due to our efforts to try to keep this book to a manageable length, we've created a link that will give you access to all of your additional bonus material.

Please visit http://www.mometrix.com/bonus948/mblex to access the information.